CLAUDIA & DOMINICA
DELICIOUS

Thank you to the following people: To our families for their boundless support in every sense—without which our dream would not have been realized. To our friends for being so encouraging and enthusiastic. To Bambina Wise for her enviable literary skills. To Danielle Huthart for her wonderful art direction and design ideas.

This cookbook could not have been possible without some best-loved recipes passed on to us from friends and family, and without the countless sources of culinary inspiration on which we have relied over the years. We have both enjoyed long love affairs with wonderful cookbooks and cookery magazines, from *Gourmet*, *Vogue Entertaining* and *House & Garden*, to Martha Stewart, Delia Smith, Gary Rhodes, and believe it or not, a really old Penguin cookery book. These have all given us a starting point for years of domestic culinary adventures as we fed our loved ones and planned dinner parties. As cooking is our passion, and not our profession, we cannot take all the credit for all of the recipes in these pages, although many were indeed created in our very own kitchens. Our aim is to share our top family favourites and our tried-and-tested entertaining staples, some of which are interpretations of existing popular recipes shared amongst friends.

Published in Hong Kong by Haven Books Limited
www.havenbooksonline.com

ISBN 978-988-18094-4-5

Copyright © Claudia Shaw-d'Auriol & Dominica Yang, 2005
www.claudiaanddominica.com

Art direction and design by Whitespace

Photography by Chris Lusher, Morgan Ommer and Patrick Poon

First printed in 2005. 2nd Edition 2006. 3rd Edition 2010.

Cover: Dominica's Onion Tart. For recipe see page 23.
Back Cover: Claudia's Pasta with Scallops. For recipe see page 53.

CLAUDIA & DOMINICA
DELICIOUS

Claudia Shaw-d'Auriol & Dominica Yang

HAVEN
world kitchen

CONTENTS

NOTES FROM THE KITCHEN
CLAUDIA DOMINICA

Every now and then I wonder what life would be like without food. Not food as sustenance, not food as nourishment, but food as pleasure, food as art, food as emotion. For me, the answer is straightforward: without food, there is no life! The union between my Austrian mother and my Chinese father married two distinct culinary traditions. Growing up amid such a fusion of flavours and aromas, is it any wonder that I embrace schnitzel and apple strudel with as much delight as *char siu* and XO sauce? My love affair with food was pre-destined!

Both my grandmothers—my Austrian Oma and my Chinese Nana—were superb cooks, as is my own mother. Cooking thus evolved into something that came naturally to me and so did entertaining. I can safely say that one of my greatest pleasures in life is cooking for family and friends. There always seems to be something cooking in my kitchen, from chocolate chip cookies for my children to a Chinese soup!

Dominica and I share the same passion for food and for cooking. Over the course of many years, we have happily entertained and fed people at our homes. As many of our guests frequently ask for recipes of the dishes they have enjoyed at our table, we decided over lunch one day to compile our favourites in this book. We hope these dishes help you create memorable meals and pleasurable feasts for you, your families and your friends.

Remember, these recipes come not just from our kitchens; they come from our hearts.

Mahlzeit, bon appetit, *sik fan*!

Cooking is one of my passions. From a young age, my parents have introduced me to a wide range of good food. My mother is a great cook and we enjoy eating! We entertained a lot at home and I was always helping in the kitchen.

The real passion started when I was living on my own in London. It began with very simple home cooking. I then ventured into different types of cuisine and baking. I was often entertaining friends and trying new recipes—I simply enjoyed cooking!

Food is now a highlight at home. We *love* our meal times together, and our three boys have grown up taking an interest in what we prepare and eat. The endless enthusiasm of my husband, Trevor, and the boys has played a great part in my love for cooking today. Cooking for friends is also a great time to laugh and share together. I have learnt over the years that meals should be stress free. There are some dishes that are complicated and worth slaving for, but in general, one should plan the menu in such a way that you feel relaxed enough to enjoy both the preparation and the meal.

It has always been my dream to produce a cookbook of my favourite recipes. It was over a casual lunch a year ago with my good friend Claudia—one of the best cooks I know—that we realized we shared the same dream!

Most of my recipes are easy and have been great successes. Some are passed on from my mother or friends and have since evolved or been adapted, and some are my own creations. So, here is our first cookbook. It is about how preparing and cooking a meal can be fun. Share our passion and joy—Happy Cooking!

FIRSTS

A DELICIOUS STARTER OPENS THE PALATE TO EVEN GREATER THINGS TO COME! DOMINICA

Crispy Duck, Watercress and Roquette Salad

East-meets-West in this dish. If you can't find confit, you can use store-bought Chinese roast duck just as successfully, in which case, I suggest you do not deep-fry the meat.

Salad
400 g (14 oz) confit duck leg
oil for deep frying
60 g (1¾ cups) watercress
60 g (3 cups) roquette (arugula)
2 spring onions, finely chopped
1 red chilli, deseeded and julienned
small bunch of fresh coriander leaves
1 cucumber, thinly sliced into rounds, to serve
4–5 pomelo segments separated, to garnish

Sauce
40 ml (2¾ tablespoons) sweet soya sauce
10 ml (2 teaspoons) light soya sauce
50 ml (3½ tablespoons) tomato ketchup
1 tablespoon honey
50 ml (3½ tablespoons) orange juice
1 tablespoon sesame oil

Dressing
50 ml (3½ tablespoons) balsamic vinegar
50 ml (3½ tablespoons) olive oil
1 tablespoon sesame oil

To make the sauce, whisk all the ingredients together.

To make the dressing, whisk all the ingredients together.

To assemble the salad, deep-fry the confit duck leg in hot oil until the skin is crisp and golden. Drain well on kitchen towels and shred meat off the bone by hand. Place in a bowl. Add enough sauce to coat the duck all over and stir until well combined. Toss the watercress, roquette, chopped spring onions, and coriander leaves with the dressing.

To serve, arrange cucumber slices in a circle on the plates. Pile salad in the centre of the cucumber. Arrange duck on top of the salad and sprinkle with pomelo and chilli pieces. Drizzle around any remaining dressing.

Serves 4–6

Crispy Salmon Cakes

A classic favourite, it can be served either as a starter or a main, depending on the portion.

Salmon Cakes
450 g (1 lb) salmon, preferably on the bone
a handful of lemon peel, parsley and bay leaf
juice of ½ lemon
225 g (8 oz) potato
a pinch of cayenne pepper
a dash of anchovy essence
15 g (1 tablespoon) butter, softened
55 ml (¼ cup) milk
4 tablespoons breadcrumbs
3 tablespoons seasoned flour
1 large egg, beaten
225 g (1 cup) butter
1 tablespoon light olive oil
salt and freshly ground pepper, to taste

Sauce
900 g (2 lbs) canned or fresh tomatoes,
drained
½ teaspoon sugar
1 tablespoon marjoram
salt and freshly ground pepper
2 tablespoons capers, drained and patted
dry (chop up half and leave the rest whole)
3 tablespoons double cream
15 g (1 tablespoon) butter, cold and diced
Worcestershire sauce, chilli sauce,
and Tabasco to taste

Pre-heat the oven to 180ºC (355ºF).

Enclose the salmon, lemon peel, parsley, bay leaf and lemon juice in a lightly buttered foil parcel. Cook in the oven for about 20 minutes, or until the salmon is just done: be careful not to overcook. Discard the foil, excess water and flavourings. Flake the salmon, removing the bones and skin.

Peel the potatoes. Cook them in boiling water until tender. Drain, purée in a food processor.

In a large mixing bowl, combine salmon, potatoes, parsley, cayenne pepper, anchovy essence and softened butter. Mix well and season to taste. Gradually add enough warm water to bind the mixture loosely. Flour your hands, then divide the mixture into 10–12 cakes, each about 5 cm (2 inch) across and 1 cm (½ inch) thick. Pat the surface of each cake smooth with a palette knife. Better still, you could prepare the cakes a day in advance and just keep them in the fridge.

When ready to cook, heat up some clarified butter or vegetable oil in a frying pan. Roll the salmon cakes in seasoned flour and dust off the excess. Brush each cake with beaten egg, then coat in breadcrumbs. Fry the salmon cakes for about 2 minutes on each side until golden brown. Remove from the pan and drain on kitchen towels.

To make the sauce, purée the tomatoes and heat up in a large saucepan. Add in sugar, marjoram and pepper to taste. Boil the sauce down to about 300 ml (1¼ cup), stirring constantly to prevent it from sticking. Pass the purée tomato mix through a fine sieve, rinse out the pan and return the purée to pan. Stir in the cream and bring to a boil. Add in the capers. Continue to simmer, letting the capers flavour the sauce. Then add in Worcestershire sauce, Tabasco and chilli sauce according to taste. When ready to serve, whisk in cold, diced butter and pour it around the salmon cakes.

Serves 6–8

Pea and Ham Soup

I was served this soup in Angkor Wat and just loved it. I am a soup fiend and begged the chef for the recipe, which I have since adapted.

250 g (1⅔ cups) fresh or frozen peas
300 g (1½ cups) green split peas (denser, so you will only need 1½ cups)
50 g (1¾ oz) pancetta
160 g (5½ oz) white onion
2 small carrots
2 stalks celery
100 g (3½ oz) smoked pork hock
2 litres (8 cups) light chicken stock
3 cloves garlic
2 bay leaves
2 sprigs thyme
a sprinkle of milk
sea salt and white pepper, to taste
a drizzle of fresh cream (optional)

Peel, wash and dice onion, celery and carrot. Finely chop pancetta. Peel and crush fresh garlic. Put all ingredients (except fresh or frozen peas, seasoning and milk) in large pot and slowly bring to a simmer, skimming the fat off the top. Cover with lid that is set slightly open. Simmer for 1½ hours until the split peas are soft.

In a separate pan boil fresh or frozen peas until just cooked. Drain. Remove smoked pork hock from soup. Purée soup in blender together with the fresh peas and pass through a sieve. Put smoked pork hock back into the soup and season with salt and white pepper. Add a little extra milk if necessary to thin the soup as desired.

Serve hot. Drizzle with a little fresh cream if desired.

Serves 8

Clam and Bean Curd in Japanese Soup

A light starter that can be made into a meal if you add more ingredients. The combination of the freshness of the shellfish in the delicate soup, mixed with the crispy pork floss and the unusual taste of the eggs makes this a unique fusion.

large Japanese clams, washed and cleaned (1–2 per person)
mussels, washed and cleaned (1–2 per person)
1 block (200 g or 7 oz) Japanese soft bean curd, cut into small cubes of 2 cm (¾ inch) and evenly distributed to individual portions
3 tablespoons Japanese *Daisho* soup base powder
1 tablespoon Japanese *Mirin*
1 tablespoon Japanese soya sauce
uzu, Japanese mandarin (if unavailable, use a dash of orange or mandarin juice)
1–2 preserved thousand-year egg, chopped to 1¼ cm (½ inch) cubes
crispy pork floss (found in Malaysian/Chinese food stores), to garnish
1 spring onion, chopped
1 sheet *nori* (Japanese seaweed), shredded
1½ litres (6 cups) water

Make soup base with 1½ litres (6 cups) water and *Daisho*. Add *Mirin*, soya sauce and a dash of *uzu* juice to taste. When ready to serve, add clams and mussels into soup and cook until shells open. Put a few small cubes of bean curd in each serving bowl. Pour in the soup, then distribute the clams and mussels. Put the egg and crispy pork floss on top. Sprinkle with spring onion, *nori* and a small twig of *uzu* rind. Serve immediately.

Serves 4

Duck and Porcini Mushroom Risotto

Risottos are not as tricky as people think. All one needs is a little patience!

600g (1 lb 5 oz) duck leg confit, meat removed from bones and shredded
3–4 tablespoons olive oil
2 small onions, peeled and diced finely
2 litres (8 cups) chicken stock
125ml (½ cup) dry white wine
500g (2½ cups) Arborio rice
40g (1½ oz) dried porcini mushrooms, soaked in warm water to soften
50g (1 cup) Parmesan cheese, finely grated
20g (1½ tablespoons) unsalted butter
2 rounded tablespoons crème fraiche
shaved Parmesan cheese, to garnish
a bunch flat-leaf parsley leaves, to garnish

Fry about 150g (5 oz) of the confit in the duck fat until crispy. Drain on kitchen towels and keep warm.

In a large stock pot or saucepan, heat the olive oil over low heat. Add the onion and cook until softened but not browned.

Meanwhile, in a separate saucepan, bring the stock to a simmer. Add the rice to the onion and toss until every grain is coated with oil then pour in the white wine, stirring to let the alcohol evaporate. Add a ladleful of the simmering stock and cook the rice, stirring constantly until the liquid is almost absorbed. Repeat the process until all the stock has been absorbed and the rice is creamy but firm to the bite (about 20 minutes). If the rice is still too firm add more stock until the rice is done. Stir in the mushrooms, the soaking liquid and the remaning duck before the final ladleful of stock.

Remove from the heat, stir in the grated parmesan, butter and crème fraiche, and season to taste. Cover the pot for a minute or so to let the rice absorb all the flavours.

Quickly spoon the risotto into small bowls, sprinkle with shaved Parmesan, parsley leaves and the crispy confit. Serve immediately.

Serves 6–8

Roquette with Roasted Tomato and Prosciutto Salad with Tangy Lemon and Brown Sugar Dressing

For a seemingly simple salad, the flavours combine surprisingly well. Perfect for a summer starter, especially when tomatoes are at their best.

Salad

12 slices prosciutto (Parma ham)
6 Roma (plum) tomatoes, halved
200 g (7 oz) roquette (arugula) or baby spinach leaves
200 g (7 oz) fresh asparagus, blanched (optional)
25 g (½ cup) Parmesan cheese shavings
a sprinkle of olive oil
a pinch of cracked black pepper

Dressing

6 tablespoons olive oil
3 tablespoons lemon juice
15 g (¼ cup) basil leaves, shredded
3 teaspoons soft brown sugar
½ teaspoon grainy mustard
½ teaspoon salt, or to taste
freshly ground black pepper

Place prosciutto and tomatoes (cut side up) in a baking dish, and sprinkle with olive oil and pepper. Bake at 180°C (355°F) for 25 minutes or until prosciutto is crisp and tomatoes are soft. Arrange spinach and asparagus on serving plates. Top with the tomatoes and prosciutto.

To make the dressing, combine all the ingredients together. Drizzle dressing over the salad and sprinkle with Parmesan shavings.

Serves 4–6

Onion Tart

Another easy and mouth-watering recipe! These tarts can be prepared in advance and then quickly heated before serving.

Pastry
110 g (1 cup) plain (all-purpose) flour
55 g (¼ cup) butter, keep cool
1 egg yolk
a pinch of salt
alternatively, use ready-made
shortcrust pastry dough

Filling
110 g (½ cup) butter
4 onions, thinly sliced half-rings
4 egg yolks
300 ml (1¼ cups) double cream
salt and pepper
2 pieces anchovies, chopped (optional)
2 pieces bacon, chopped (optional)

Pre-heat the oven to 170°C (340°F).

Sift flour with a pinch of salt. Cut butter into small cubes in the flour so the cubes are coated with flour, and rub through flour with your finger tips, until the mixture resembles fine breadcrumbs. Make a valley in the centre of the mixture and beat in the egg with a fork. Use a wooden spoon to bind the mixture into a dough, then your hands to knead the dough. Wrap the dough and set aside in fridge for 20–30 minutes.

When ready to bake the pastry, take the dough from the fridge and thinly roll out the pastry into small tartlet trays (I suggest 9–10 cm (3½–4 inch) diameter containers). Use a small fork to pierce the bottom of the pastry a couple of times to prevent air trapping while baking. Line each tartlet tray with a piece of greaseproof paper and fill with some uncooked rice or dry beans. Bake the tartlets blind for 20 minutes, removing the greaseproof paper and rice or beans in the last 5 minutes. Remove tartlets and cool, keeping them in the trays.

Note: the pastry dough can be made the day before and kept in the refrigerator. Leave it out at room temperature for 30 minutes before rolling. The tartlets can also be baked earlier and stored in an airtight container.

For the filling, melt butter gently in a deep frying pan, add in the sliced onions and mix well. Sweat the onions on a low heat with the pan covered until the onions soften but are not browning. Remove the lid and keep stewing until all liquid evaporates. Set aside and cool.

Beat the egg yolks and mix in the cream. Add to the onions with salt and plenty of pepper. If you wish, add in chopped anchovies and/or bacon. Mix well.

Fill the pastry shells up to 1 hour before cooking. Take the individual pastries out of the trays and place them onto a large baking tray. Fill the tartlets generously. Bake them at 180°C (355°F) for 40 minutes, until the tops are golden brown. Alternatively, bake one large tart, using an 20 cm (8 inch) flan tin and slice it into individual portions.

Serves 6

Caviar d'Aubergine

I have no idea why this is called caviar d'aubergine but it often forms part of our summer lunches when we are in France. It is basically a thick purée of eggplant, tomato and olive oil. It's delicious eaten on its own or served with warm pita bread. It can be served as part of a mezze platter with hummous and tabbouleh.

2 large aubergines (eggplants)
4 cloves garlic
6 tablespoons olive oil
2 teaspoons peppercorns
2 small sticks of cinnamon
1 large tomato, deseeded and diced
1 shallot, finely chopped
2 tablespoons crème fraiche or double cream

2 teaspoons sherry vinegar
5 g (2 tablespoons) mint, finely chopped
5 g (2 tablespoons) Italian parsley, finely chopped
3 tablespoons chives, finely chopped
juice of ½ lemon
a dash of balsamic vinegar
a dash of *fleur de sel*
salt and pepper to taste

Pre-heat the oven to 200°C (390°F).

Peel 2 garlic cloves and cut in half lengthwise, take out the green root and slice into narrow sticks. Wash the aubergines and make small incisions into the skin. Place the garlic sticks inside the incisions. Place each aubergine on a piece of aluminium foil, drizzle each with 1 tablespoon olive oil and sprinkle with salt. Add 1 teaspoon peppercorns and 1 small stick of cinnamon to each and wrap up. Place on a baking tray and bake for 1½ hours.

Peel and finely chop the remaining cloves of garlic. Cut the cooked aubergine in half lengthwise, scoop out the pulp and chop finely, or mash with fork.

In a pan, heat 1 tablespoon olive oil, add the shallot and garlic and fry until soft. Add the diced tomato. Mix and de-glaze the pan with the sherry vinegar. Add the aubergine and cook until the liquid has evaporated. Take off the heat and season with salt, pepper and lemon juice to taste. Slowly add the crème fraiche or double cream and a tablespoon of olive oil. Leave to cool.

Once cooled to room temperature, mix the mint, parsley and chives into the aubergine and add more lemon juice to taste. To serve, sprinkle with *fleur de sel* and drizzle with olive oil and a few drops of balsamic vinegar. Sprinkle some extra chopped parsley on top.

Makes a large bowl as part of a mezze platter, or to serve as an hors d'oeuvre with drinks.

Serves 8

Herbed Pancakes with Mascarpone and Smoked Salmon

An alternative way to serve smoked salmon. This can be served as a starter, as a light meal or even for a lazy Sunday morning brunch.

150 g (1⅓ cups) self-raising flour
2 tablespoons chives, chopped
2 tablespoons dill, chopped
2 tablespoons Italian parsley, chopped
1 egg, lightly beaten
200 ml (¾ cup) milk
3 tablespoons lemon juice
30 g (2¼ tablespoons) butter, melted
60 ml (¼ cup) mascarpone cheese
60 ml (¼ cup) crème fraiche
1 teaspoon prepared horseradish
freshly ground black pepper, to taste
a pinch of salt
200 g (7 oz) Scottish smoked salmon
lemon wedges and sprigs of dill, to serve

Combine flour, herbs and salt in a bowl and make a well in the centre of the mixture. Whisk together egg and milk, then slowly add to the well of mixture, whisking constantly to gradually incorporate flour. Whisk in 2 tablespoons of lemon juice. Stir in melted butter. Season to taste with salt and cracked pepper and whisk until batter is smooth.

Heat a little extra butter in a heavy-based frying pan and cook 2 tablespoons of mixture at a time for 2 minutes each side, or until golden. Transfer to a warm oven while cooking the remaining pancakes.

Combine mascarpone cheese, crème fraiche, 1 tablespoon of lemon juice and prepared horseradish in a bowl, season to taste with freshly ground pepper and whisk until well combined.

To serve, place a warmed pancake on each plate, top with a spoonful of mascarpone mixture and a slice of smoked salmon and repeat layering once more. Then scatter with extra sprigs of dill. Serve immediately with lemon wedges.

Serves 6

Scrambled Eggs with Char Siu on Brioche

This is one of our family's favourites: we call it comfort food.

60 g (½ cup) spring onion (scallions), chopped
400 g (14 oz) *char siu* (Chinese barbecued pork) — try and get half fat/half lean, thin slices
Ask the roast meat shop for some of the roast juices (about ½ cup)
6–8 eggs, beaten with a little seasoning
vegetable oil
4 brioches
4 sprigs of corriander, to serve

Heat up a non-stick frying pan and coat with vegetable oil. Gently fry the spring onion. Add in the *char siu*, let the fat turn a little glazy. Increase the heat. Pour in the roast juices, then gently stir in the egg mixture. Let the bottom start to brown and set a little, mixing in the meat and spring onion. Brown slightly but maintain a moist and runny consistency, making sure not to overcook.

Meanwhile, warm up the brioche in the oven. Open each brioche vertically down the middle and place on a plate. Divide up the egg mixture and serve over the centre of each brioche with a sprig of coriander. Alternatively, eat it the Chinese way — served on a big plate with rice and other dishes.

Serves 4

Mini Shrimp Toast

A classic Chinese favourite. Serve it as starter, canapé or a simple snack.

350 g (12 oz) shrimps
4 pieces sliced white bread
1 egg white
1–2 tablespoons diced onion (optional)
1 small bunch parsley leaves, finely chopped
⅓ teaspoon salt
1 egg white or 2 tablespoons of egg white
1 teaspoon corn flour
a dash of sesame oil
a pinch of pepper
a few drops of Worcestershire sause, to serve
lettuce leaves, to serve

Trim crusts off bread and cut diagonally into 4 triangles. Remove intestines from shrimps, rinse well and wipe dry. Mash shrimps and stir in the egg white, corn flour and diced onion. Mix well to a sticky consistency. Spread a generous portion of shrimp paste over each piece of bread, and sprinkle parsley leaves over. Place all the shrimp toast into hot oil and fry until golden brown and crispy.

Remove from oil, soak up excess oil and drain on kitchen towels. Sprinkle with a few drops of Worcestershire sauce. Serve shrimp toast on a bed of lettuce.

Serves 4

Crab and Cauliflower Cappuccino

A wonderful soup which can be dressed up with a generous spoon of caviar.

65g (4½ tablespoons) butter, chopped
1 onion, chopped
1 leek, chopped
2 cloves of garlic, finely chopped
1 fresh bay leaf
2 sprigs of thyme
1 litre (4 cups) chicken stock
500ml (2 cups) milk
350g (12 oz) cauliflower (about ½ head), cut into florets
180g (6½ oz) cooked crab meat, picked through
caviar, to serve (optional)
sea salt and freshly ground black pepper, to taste

Melt butter in a heavy-based saucepan, add onion, leek and garlic and cook over medium heat for 5–6 minutes or until soft. Add bay leaf, thyme, chicken stock, milk and cauliflower. Bring to boil, then reduce heat to low and simmer for 15–20 minutes or until cauliflower is tender.

Process cauliflower mixture in a food processor or blender until smooth, then strain through a sieve. Season to taste with some sea salt and freshly ground black pepper. Add hot stock or milk if the soup is too thick.

Divide crab meat between cups or small bowls. Using a hand-held blender, froth soup in batches, then pour into cups. Spoon a little caviar on top if desired.

Serves 6

Crab Meat Terrine

A light, easy summer starter—a great alternative to crabmeat cocktail. The lemongrass and chilli give it a subtle Asian twist.

Terrine
400g (14 oz) canned crab meat, strained
2 stalks of lemongrass, finely chopped
2 small tomatoes, deseeded, finely chopped & strained
1 small chilli, deseeded and finely chopped
25g (1¾ tablespoons) mayonnaise
25g (1¾ tablespoons) sour cream
salt and pepper, to taste
2 ripe avocados
juice of ½ lime
½ tablespoon coriander leaves
1 stalk of spring onion (scallions), finely chopped
½ tablespoon extra virgin olive oil
salt, to taste

Sauce
225g (8 oz) canned or fresh tomatoes, drained
½ teaspoon sugar
salt and pepper, to taste
2 tablespoons double cream
a dash of Worcestershire sauce, balsamic vinegar and Tabasco sauce
crab roe, to garnish
mixed salad leaves, to serve

Combine the crab meat, lemongrass, tomatoes, chilli, mayonnaise and sour cream together. Add salt to taste. Set aside in fridge. Mash avocado roughly with lime juice and coriander. Set aside in fridge.

You may assemble the terrines ½ hour to 1 hour before serving. Drain any liquid from the mixtures. Use metal rings about 5–6cm (2–2½ inch)-deep and 6cm (2½ inch) in diameter. Place the rings on a flat plate or baking tray. Fill the bottom of each ring with 2 tablespoons of the avocado mixture and gently pat it flat. Then lay 2 tablespoons of the crab meat mixture, again gently patting the top level. Repeat until you use up all the mixtures. Set aside in fridge.

To make the sauce, purée the tomatoes and heat in a large saucepan. Add in sugar, salt and pepper to taste. Boil the sauce down to about 150ml (1 cup) stirring constantly to prevent it from sticking. Pass the purée tomato mix through a fine sieve, rinse out the pan and return the purée to pan. Stir in the cream and bring to a boil. Continue to simmer. Add in Worcestershire sauce, balsamic vinegar and Tabasco sauce. Cool and set side until ready to use.

To serve, simply slide a spatula under each terrine, put them gently onto the plates and remove the rings. Garnish with some crab roe and salad leaves. Serve the sauce around the terrines.

Serves 4

Chinese Turnip Cake

This is a traditional dish for the Chinese New Year but one could eat it all year round. The steamed cake may be kept in the fridge for ten days. Simply fry it up whenever you wish!

These are rough measurements. The idea is 3-part turnip to 1-part rice flour.
The amount of other ingredients is a matter of personal preference.

1.35 kg (3 lbs) turnip
1 small piece ginger
450 g (1 lb) rice flour
3 wind-dried pork or beef sausages
3 wind-dried liver sausages
2 sticks wind dried fatty pork
4 dried scallops, soaked and softened
6 dried Chinese mushrooms, soaked and softened
2 pieces spring onion (scallions)
a small bunch of coriander
2 tablespoons light soya sauce
1 tablespoon sugar
2 tablespoons Chinese Xiao Shing wine
sesame seeds and sprigs of coriander, to garnish
oyster sauce or chilli sauce, to serve

Shred the turnip by hand or by using an electric shredder. Put the turnip shreds in a large pot. Add the piece of ginger and cook on medium heat until the turnip softens and you can the smell its sweetness (in about 20 minutes). Depending on the freshness of the turnip, the amount of liquid released may vary.

Chop all ingredients into small cubes. Heat oil in a frying pan and gently fry the chopped ingredients. Add a moderate seasoning of light soya sauce, sugar and Chinese Xiao Shing wine. Set aside and cool.

When turnip has softened, slowly mix in the rice flour until it has the consistency of a wet paste. Then slowly stir in the chopped ingredients. Mix well.

Put the mixture in a 5 cm (2 inch)-deep, 25 cm (10 inch) cake tin. The above quantities will fill two cake tins of this size. Steam for 40 minutes. Sprinkle the top of the cake with sesame seeds and a few sprigs of coriander. The cake will keep in the fridge for 1 week.

To cook, roughly slice the turnip cake into 5 x 4 x 1 cm (2 x 1½ x ½ inch) pieces, and steam or pan-fry them. Serve with a dollop of oyster or chilli sauce if desired.

Serves 10–12

Minty Zucchini Fritters with Horseradish and Yoghurt Sauce

Perfect to serve as a light lunch.

Fritters
500 g (1 lb 2 oz) zucchini, grated
8 spring onions (scallions), chopped
125 g (¾ cup) feta or ricotta cheese, crumbled
10 g (⅓ cup) Italian parsley, chopped
5 g (2 tablespoons) mint, chopped
2 tablespoons thyme
2 eggs, lightly beaten
60 g (½ cup) plain (all-purpose) flour
60 ml (¼ cup) olive oil for shallow frying
salt and freshly ground black pepper

Sauce
60 ml (¼ cup) plain yoghurt
60 ml (¼ cup) crème fraiche
juice of ½ lemon
1 teaspoon prepared horseradish
1 teaspoon Dijon mustard
2 tablespoons chives, chopped
salt and freshly ground black pepper

For the sauce, place all the ingredients in bowl and stir to mix.

For the fritters, mix zucchini, spring onion, feta or ricotta, parsley, mint, thyme and eggs together lightly in a bowl. Stir in the flour, add salt and pepper to taste.

Heat the oil in a non-stick frying pan over medium to high heat. Drop rounded tablespoons of batter into the hot oil and gently flatten. Cook for 2 minutes on each side or until golden brown. Drain on kitchen towels and serve with yoghurt sauce.

Makes 20 fritters

Mussels in Coconut Cream

These mussels in a light curry are simply sensational! The sauce can be prepared in advance. Just add the mussels ten minutes before serving.

30–36 small to medium mussels
2½ cm (1 inch)-cube fresh ginger, peeled and coarsely chopped
8 cloves of garlic, peeled
300 ml (1¼ cups) water
4 tablespoons vegetable oil
200 g (1¼ cups) onions, peeled and chopped
1–2 fresh green chillies, sliced into fine shreds (select the hot ones, for extra spice)
½ teaspoon turmeric
2 teaspoons ground cumin
250 ml–500 ml (1–2 cups) coconut milk
½ teaspoon salt
a few sprigs of coriander leaves, to garnish

Wash and scrub the mussels clean.

Put the ginger and garlic in a blender, add 100 ml (½ cup) water and blend until smooth. Set aside. Put oil in a large pan over medium heat. When hot, add onions and sauté until they become translucent. Add in paste from the blender, green chillies, turmeric and cumin. Stir fry for a couple of minutes, then add the coconut milk, salt and 200 ml (¾ cup) water. Bring to a boil. Add seasoning and coconut milk to taste. The sauce can be made several hours in advance.

When ready to serve, heat up the sauce. When bubbling, add in mussels and cover tightly. Turn heat to medium and let mussels steam for about 6–10 minutes, until they open up. Discard any mussels that fail to open.

Serve immediately in a low (pasta) bowl with some fresh, crusty bread. Garnish the dish with a few sprigs of coriander.

Serves 6

Seared Scallops on a Trio of Vegetables

This was inspired by a dish I had in Sydney, where they served the scallops on a few slices of Spanish chorizo. Here, I use the Chinese wind-dried liver sausage which adds a different dimension to the palate.

1 carrot, finely shredded
1 stick of celery, finely shredded
1 cucumber, finely shredded
24–32 scallops, depending on the size
2–3 Chinese wind-dried liver sausage, sliced diagonally to 6 mm (¼ inch) thick
a dash of balsamic vinegar
a dash of extra-virgin olive oil
salt and pepper

Blanch the shredded carrot and celery in hot, salted water. Drain and set aside. When cool, mix well together with the cucumber to form a colourful trio. Set aside.

Make sure scallops are at room temperature. When ready to cook, heat up a skillet pan. Coat with olive oil. Meanwhile, place the sausage slices under the grill for 3–4 minutes to cook and release the fat. When oil is hot, add scallops and sear 1 minute on each side.

Put a small mound of shredded vegetables on each serving plate. Line 3–4 pieces of sliced sausage on the bed of vegetables and arrange the scallops on top. Sprinkle generously with salt and black pepper. Drizzle a little olive oil and balsamic vinegar over the scallops and around the plate. Serve immediately.

Serves 6

Crab Salad with Mint, Coriander and Chilli Dressing

The title says it all: a mixture of flavours typical of the East.

Salad
110g (4 oz) white crab meat per person
a selection of salad leaves
a sprinkle of olive oil
a spinkle of lemon juice

Dressing
5g (2 tablespoons) coriander leaves
5g (2 tablespoons) mint leaves
1 tablespoon palm sugar
1 green chilli, deseeded
4 tablespoons fish sauce
½ clove garlic
90ml (⅓ cup) water
juice of 2 limes

To make the dressing, place all the dressing ingredients in a food processor and pulse until they have formed a bright green sauce. Taste to see whether the sauce is spicy enough; it should have a bite but not be completely overpowering. Set aside (the dressing can be made up to 2 days in advance, but will lose its bright and vibrant colour).

For the salad, use a selection of pretty salad leaves which are not so powerful in flavour that they clash with the dressing. Toss the salad leaves in a little good-quality olive oil and lemon juice. Season and place a small pile in the centre of the plate. Toss the crab meat in a touch of olive oil and drizzle generously with the chilli-mint dressing. Place a mound of the dressed crab on top of the salad leaves and serve immediately.

Serves 6–8

Ultimate Cheese Lovers' Tart

I serve this with a fresh herb and tomato salad with chutney on the side.

Pastry
175g (1¾ cups) plain flour
a pinch of ground paprika
75g (⅓ cup) butter
75g (⅔ cup) mature cheddar cheese, grated
3 tablespoons cold water
a pinch of salt and pepper

Filling
3 eggs, separated
280ml (1¼ cups) single cream
2 teaspoons Dijon mustard
150g (1⅓ cups) gruyère cheese, grated
50g (⅓ cup) feta cheese, crumbled
125g (1 cup) brie or camembert, de-rinded and cut into 1cm (½ inch) cubes

Pre-heat the oven to 220°C (430°F).

Sift flour, paprika and salt into a large bowl. Cut butter into the flour mixture and rub it in with fingertips until the mixture resembles fine breadcrumbs. Stir in the cheddar and bind with 3 tablespoons of cold water. Chill the dough for 30 minutes. Alternatively, you can make the dough in a food processor.

Roll the dough out to line a 3cm (1 inch)-deep, 23cm (9 inch) loose-based flan tin. Prick the base and chill for another 30 minutes. Line the flan tin with foil or baking paper and fill with pie weights or dried beans. Bake 15 minutes. Remove the beans and paper, prick the pastry and return to oven for another 10–15 minutes or until lightly browned.

Whisk together yolks, cream, mustard and seasonings. Stir in the gruyère, feta and brie or camembert cubes. Whisk the egg whites until stiff but not dry, and fold into the cream mixture. Pour into the pastry case and bake for 30–40 minutes or until set. Cool for 15 minutes and serve.

Serves 8

Sashimi Terrine with Lime and Coriander Sauce

A fusion inspiration which is very easy and stress-free to prepare. The sauce is adapted from my friend Wendy's recipe, and is an excellent sauce to go with any plain fish dish.

Terrine
110g tuna sashimi
110g salmon sashimi
2 tablespoons spring onion, finely chopped
3 tablespoons white Japanese radish, slightly pickled
3 tablespoons *wo ju sun* (Shanghainese asparagus), chopped, can be substituted with cooked asparagus
nori (Japanese seaweed), thinly shredded, to garnish
ikura (Japanese salmon roe), to garnish

Sauce
175g (¾ cup) unsalted butter
60g (½ cup) spring onion (scallions), finely chopped
60g (1 cup) coriander, finely chopped
½ tablespoon lime juice
1 tablespoon Japanese soya sauce
wasabi (Japanese mustard), to taste

You can prepare the terrine up to 1 day in advance, but make sure the sashimi is fresh — handle as little as possible with your hands and do it in a cool area.

Chop the tuna into a fine mince. Next, chop the salmon into a fine mince and mix in the spring onion. Set aside both the minced tuna and salmon separately in the fridge to keep cool. Chop the radish and asparagus separately into tiny cubes and set aside.

Brush 8 small ramekin dishes lightly with vegetable oil. Line the bottom of each ramekin with a layer of minced tuna, followed by a layer of chopped asparagus, then a layer of minced salmon, and finally by a layer of chopped radish. Make sure you pack in each layer tightly; they need to be pressed down and the layers level. Cover the ramekins with cling film and set aside in the refrigerator.

To make the sauce, melt butter slowly in saucepan. Add in the spring onion and coriander, turning down heat. Add in the lime juice and soya sauce. Turn off the heat. Add *wasabi* to taste.

Note: the sauce is now ready; only re-heat briefly just before serving to avoid overcooking the coriander and spring onion.

When ready to serve, remove the ramekins from the fridge. Using a small, sharp knife, gently slice round the edge of the terrine. Turn the terrines out onto their individual plates — the ramekins might need a little pat on the bottom. Gently heat the sauce and pour generously around the edge of each terrine. Sprinkle the tops with thinly shredded *nori* and a little salmon roe. Serve immediately and enjoy!

Serves 4

SECONDS

THERE'S ONLY ONE GOLDEN RULE: USE ONLY THE FRESHEST INGREDIENTS YOU CAN FIND. CLAUDIA

Taglierini with Caramelised Scallops and Rosemary Beurre Blanc

A wonderful combination of seafood and pasta.

Pasta
500 g (1 lb 2 oz) good-quality dried taglierini or fettuccine
500–700 g (1–1½ lbs) sea scallops

Beurre Blanc
125 ml (½ cup) dry white wine
2 tablespoons white-wine vinegar
60 g (¼ cup) shallot, chopped
1 tablespoon garlic, chopped
2 teaspoons fresh rosemary leaves, chopped
3 tablespoons crème fraiche or 125 ml (½ cup) double cream
110 g (½ cup) cold unsalted butter, cut into pieces
salt and pepper, to taste
2 tablespoons vegetable oil
fresh rosemary and parsley leaves, chopped, to garnish
grated zest of 1 lemon

For the beurre blanc, simmer wine, vinegar, shallot, garlic and rosemary in a heavy saucepan until reduced to about 2 tablespoons. Add cream and simmer until liquid is reduced by half. Add all the butter and cook over moderately low heat, swirling pan constantly, until just creamy and the butter is incorporated. Do not let it boil (the sauce must not get hot enough to liquefy: it should be the consistency of hollandaise). Remove pan from heat and add salt and pepper to taste.

Discard tough muscle from side of each scallop if necessary. Pat scallops dry and season with salt and pepper. In a heavy frying pan, heat 1 tablespoon oil over moderately high heat until hot but not smoking, Arrange half of scallops, without crowding, in skillet and cook undisturbed for 1–2 minutes, or until undersides are golden brown. Turn scallops over and repeat. Transfer scallops to a bowl and keep warm. Cook the rest of the scallops in remaining amount of oil in the same manner.

Cook pasta in boiling salted water until al dente (about 15 minutes for fresh, longer for dried) and drain. Transfer pasta to a heated bowl and pour sauce through a fine sieve onto pasta. Add any liquid accumulated in bowl of scallops and toss.

Divide pasta among 6 heated plates. Arrange scallops on top of pasta and garnish with herbs and a little lemon zest.

Serves 6

Inche Kabin: Mum's Malaysian Chicken

Just a very simple dish, but the spices make it special.

8–10 chicken pieces (wings, thighs and drumsticks)
½ tablespoon *ketumber* (coriander) powder
1 teaspoon *jintan puteh* (cumin) powder
1 teaspoon *jintan manis* (fennel) powder
1 tablespoon *kunjit* (saffron) powder
½ teaspoon pepper
2 teaspoons salt
1 tablespoon sugar
1 tablespoon lemon juice
1 tablespoon Chinese light soya sauce

Put chicken pieces into a mixing bowl. Add in all the above ingredients for the marinade. Mix well. Rub and brush into the chicken, under the skin and bone. Leave for a couple of hours or longer—even overnight.

When ready to serve, deep-fry the chicken pieces until brown and crispy around the skin. If you prefer, you may grill or barbeque the chicken, which is equally tasty. Serve with hot rice or a salad.

Serves 4

Pasta with Fresh Tomato Sauce, Roasted Proscuitto and Parmesan Cream

This is a staple in my household. You can vary the pasta by adding sautéed pieces of chicken or asparagus. The creamy parmesan sauce adds a wonderful dimension to all the flavours.

600g (1 lb 5 oz) Roma (plum) or vine tomatoes, roughly chopped
15g (1 tablespoon) unsalted butter
1 tablespoon olive oil
1 tablespoon sugar (adjust depending on how sweet the tomatoes are)
1 tablespoon tomato paste (again adjust depending how flavourful the tomatoes are)
300g (⅔ lb) dried pasta such as penne, pappardelle or spaghetti
150ml (⅔ cup) carton single cream
50g (1 cup) Parmesan cheese, freshly grated
50g (1¾ oz) proscuitto (Parma ham), thinly sliced
salt and ground black pepper
fresh basil, to serve
olive oil or butter, to serve

Heat butter and olive oil in frying pan. When hot, add tomatoes, sugar, tomato paste, salt and pepper. Cook until the liquid has evaporated and you have a rich tomato sauce.

Cook the pasta in boiling salted water until just tender. Drain well.

Whilst the pasta is cooking, place the cream in a small saucepan with half the cheese. Heat until just boiling. Keep stirring to get a nice, creamy consistency.

Roast the prosciutto slices in the oven until crisp. Place on kitchen towels to absorb oil. Set aside.

Toss the pasta with a good splash of extra virgin olive oil or knob of butter and add the remaining cheese. Divide pasta on individual plates, spoon over some tomato sauce and drizzle with the Parmesan cream. Finish off with a slice or two of roasted prosciutto and sprinkle with torn pieces of fresh basil and freshly ground black pepper. Serve immediately.

Serves 4

Kazi's Sticky Barbecued Ribs

I tasted these sticky ribs at my great friend Kazi's house and knew I had to have this recipe. I love ribs and these ones are amazing!

Ribs
2 racks baby back pork ribs (about 2½ kg or 5½ lbs in total), cut into 2 rib pieces
125 ml (½ cup) vinegar
water, to boil ribs

Sauce
250 ml (1 cup) tomato ketchup
125 ml (½ cup) water
125 ml (½ cup) dark soya sauce
180 g (½ cup) honey
2 cloves garlic, peeled and crushed

Place spare ribs in saucepan with vinegar and add enough water to cover the ribs. Bring to a boil. Reduce heat and simmer, skimming off froth, for 1 hour. Drain ribs well and pat dry.

To make the sauce, place all the sauce ingredients into a pan and simmer for 1 hour until you get a thick rich sauce. Coat ribs well in sauce and place on a foil-lined broiler pan, rounded side up. Roast under the grill about 30 minutes until ribs are tender and glaze is well browned (the sugar in the sauce burns easily so keep watching the grill).

Delicious served with corn on the cob, mashed or baked potatoes and a salad. Perfect for a summer meal.

Serves 6

Mum's Laksa

Another HIT! This is an old recipe from my mother, who spent part of her childhood in Kuala Lumpur. An all-time favourite—it never fails to satisfy.

The following ingredients are just a guideline. I normally allow at least 2–3 prawns per serving, 2 fishballs, 2–3 slices of fishcake, etc.

Fresh ingredients
125 ml (½ cup) oil
500 ml (2 cups) coconut cream
500 ml (2 cups) coconut milk
500 ml (2 cups) fish stock, or stock made from prawns
12–18 prawns, shelled
12–18 fishballs and fishcakes, sliced
1 cooked white chicken from the Chinese roast-meat shop, (or just plain poached or cooked chicken), shredded
600 g (1 lb 5 oz) *lai fun* or *mei fun* (vermicelli)
175 g (6 oz) bean sprouts
12–18 dry bean curd square puffs
1 green cucumber, cut into thin sticks
salt to taste

Ground ingredients
6 slices *lengkuas* (Thai ginger)
6 *buah keras* (candlenuts)
½ teaspoon *kunjit* (saffron) powder
2 teaspoons roasted *ketumber* (coriander) powder
1 square of *belachan* (shrimp paste)
2 stalks lemongrass, thinly sliced
5 fresh chillies, deseeded
1 teaspoon chilli powder
75 g (½ cup) shallots, chopped and deep-fried, to garnish

Put ½ cup of oil in a deep pan, when hot add all ground ingredients and fry until well cooked. Add in the prawns and ½ teaspoon salt and fry for 5 minutes, then add in the coconut milk and stock. When it boils, take out the prawns and set aside. Add in the coconut cream and keep stirring until it boils again, then remove from the heat immediately. Adjust thickness and taste according to personal preference. The thickness varies each time due to the coconut milk.

Just before serving, blanch the *lai fun* or *mei fun*, and the bean sprouts separately. Set aside. Put the remaining fresh ingredients in the laksa to soak in the soup a little and warm up. Distribute in individual bowls, sprinkle with fried shallots and serve immediately.

Alternatively, put the cooked *lai fun* or *mei fun* in the serving bowl, then add fresh ingredients. Pour in the hot soup, then sprinkle the fried shallots on top and serve. Be generous with the soup as all the ingredients must be submerged!

Serves 6

Chicken Roasted with Rosemary and Garlic

A delicious dish of chicken joints cooked on a bed of sliced red onions with whole cloves of garlic and fresh rosemary sprigs. An alternative to the traditional roast chicken.

Chicken
2 red onions, peeled and thinly sliced
1.6 kg (3–3½ lbs) oven-ready chicken, cut into 8 pieces
12 whole garlic cloves, unpeeled
2–3 sprigs fresh rosemary
4 tablespoons olive oil
sea salt and freshly ground black pepper

Sauce
a generous splash of red wine
1 generous tablespoon crème fraiche
a dash of soya sauce
½ teaspoon sugar

Pre-heat the oven to 200°C (390°F).

Spread onion slices in the bottom of a large roasting tray. Sit the chicken pieces on top. Scatter over garlic cloves and rosemary. Drizzle over oil and season chicken with sea salt and black pepper. Roast in a pre-heated oven for 10 minutes until beginning to brown, then lower heat to 180°C (355°F). Continue cooking for 45 minutes or until chicken pieces are cooked through and browned and onions are caramelised.

Arrange the chicken on a platter with onions, garlic and remove rosemary. Pour red wine into the roasting pan and stir to scrape up sediment and any remaining juices. Add the crème fraiche. Over medium heat, bring the sauce to the boil, adding the soya sauce and a pinch of sugar to taste. Drizzle over chicken before serving.

Serves 4

Sole Fillets with Tomato and Caper Sauce

This dish would work well with any fish and is delicious served with pasta.

30 g (½ cup) Italian parsley, chopped
2 tablespoons capers, rinsed and lightly chopped
125 ml (½ cup) olive oil, for frying
5–6 tomatoes, deseeded and diced
1 tablespoon tomato paste
salt and pepper, to taste
6 skinless sole fillets (they should be a good size)
60 g (½ cup) plain (all-purpose) flour
120 g (½ cup) butter
1 tablespoon lemon juice
60 ml (¼ cup) white wine
1 teaspoon sugar
1 tablespoon Worcestershire sauce

Pre-heat the oven to 230°C (445°F).

Combine the parsley and capers in a bowl.

In a large pan, heat olive oil until hot and sauté tomatoes and tomato paste for a few minutes until slightly thickened and cooked. Season to taste; make sure it is not too salty as the fish is also seasoned. Set aside.

Salt and pepper the fillets and then cover in flour. Shake off the excess flour. In a cleaned frying pan, heat a little olive oil until very hot, and brown the fillets on both sides in batches. Transfer the browned fillets to a shallow baking dish. Spoon the cooked tomatoes onto the fish.

In the same pan in which the fish was cooked, melt the butter, add the lemon juice, white wine, the sugar and Worcestershire sauce. Make sure all the brown bits are scraped up. Cook until slightly reduced, then add the capers and parsley and adjust seasoning. Pour over the fish. Bake in the oven for 5–10 minutes, until the fish is thoroughly cooked. Serve immediately.

Serves 6

Duck Breast with Soba

The delicate flavour of the soba and mushrooms really complements the rich taste of the duck. This is a classic method of preparing duck breast. You may improvise with other sauces such as orange, cherry, honey and lime, etc.

4 duck breasts
salt and pepper
4 tablespoons Japanese BBQ sauce (if you cannot find, add a little Kikkoman
soya sauce, sugar and *Mirin* to a standard mild BBQ sauce)
1 tablespoon Chinese chilli bean paste
400 g (14 oz) soba (Japanese buckwheat noodles)
250 ml (1 cup) bottled soba sauce
150 g (5 oz) assorted Japanese mushrooms
oil, to sauté mushroom

Pre-heat the oven to 190ºC (375ºF).

Score the skin of the duck breast with a sharp knife making a criss-cross pattern, but do not cut down to the meat. Season generously with salt and pepper. Put a heavy frying pan on high heat. Place in the duck breast, skin down (no need for oil). Let the oil slowly drizzle out from the duck skin and the skin burn down until it turns golden brown. If too much oil is released, remove some from the pan. Set the duck aside skin upwards. Brush breast with BBQ sauce mixed with chilli-bean paste. Roast breast in oven at 190ºC (375ºF) for 15–20 minutes (depending on how pink you like it).

Cook soba noodles according to instructions on package. When ready, drain the noodles, pour in the soba sauce and mix well. Let the duck breasts sit for 5 minutes, then slice into thin, diagonal pieces. When ready to serve, distribute soba noodles to plates. Arrange the sliced duck breasts on top. Serve over a bed of warm soba and some sautéed Japanese mushrooms. When arranging the duck slices, be sure to brush on some of the lovely juices from the baking tray!

Alternatively, you could sauté the mushrooms in a little vegetable oil with some chopped garlic, then add in the soba noodles and stir well with enough sauce to flavour the ingredients.

Serves 4

Lamb Meat Loaf with Fresh Tomato Salsa

This is an absolute favourite for boat trips; easy to make and so tasty.

Meat Loaf
1 medium onion, peeled and chopped
2–3 cloves garlic, peeled and chopped
80 ml (⅓ cup) tomato ketchup
125 g (4 oz) pancetta, rind removed and chopped
500 g (1 lb 2 oz) lean lamb, minced
250 g (9 oz) chicken, minced
2 tablespoons Worcestershire sauce
80 g (⅓ cup) fresh breadcrumbs
1 large egg
1 teaspoon rosemary, chopped
1 tablespoon dried or fresh marjoram
salt and cracked pepper, to taste
4 rashers pancetta or bacon, de-rinded
a sprig of rosemary

Salsa
5 vine tomatoes, diced
1 small red onion, finely chopped
2 tablespoons fresh lemon thyme
6 tablespoons olive oil
2 tablespoons balsamic vinegar
1 teaspoon salt or to taste
fresh ground pepper

Pre-heat the oven to 200°C (390°F).

Mix all the meat loaf ingredients together (except sprig of rosemary and the rashers of pancetta) by hand until completely incorporated. Place the mixture in a loaf pan. Place a sprig of rosemary on the meat loaf and lay the pancetta or bacon slices on top. Cook on centre shelf of the oven for 45 minutes to 1 hour.

In the meantime, prepare the salsa by combining all the ingredients together in a bowl.

Serve lamb loaf hot or cold with the salsa. Lamb meat loaves are also delicious cold with a green salad or in sandwiches, with chutney.

Serves 6–8

Monkfish in a Saffron-Flavoured Tomato Sauce

You can use any type of fish really, but monkfish works well because it retains its shape during cooking.

1 kg (2 lb 4 oz) monkfish, cut into large cubes
2 carrots
2 medium-sized onions finely chopped
2 tablespoons cognac
2 teaspoons plain (all-purpose) flour
150 ml (⅔ cup) white wine
100 ml (⅓ cup) fish stock (chicken stock will do too)
1 rounded tablespoon tomato paste
1 bouquet garni
a twig of fresh thyme
a pinch of saffron
150 g (⅔ cup) crème fraiche
30 g (2 tablespoons) butter
1 tablespoon olive oil
salt and pepper, to taste
rice, cooked in butter, to serve

Peel and dice the carrots and onions.

Heat the butter and olive oil in a large frying pan and sauté carrots and onions until lightly golden. Remove from pan and set aside.

In the same pan fry the monkfish pieces until golden. Add a little more olive oil if needed. Pour away any water that may have come from the fish, add vegetables to the frying pan with the fish and heat through. Pour in the cognac and flambé the monkfish. Dust with flour, add the white wine and stock. Season to taste and add the tomato paste, bouquet garni, thyme and a pinch of saffron. Stir gently to mix through. Cook on a moderate heat for 15 minutes uncovered.

Just before serving gently add the crème fraiche (be careful not to break up the fish pieces when stirring) and heat through. Serve immediately with hot buttered rice.

Serves 6

Stuffed Quail with Wild Rice

This is not a recipe for those who do not like working with their hands. It is a dish to truly impress your guests, so if you can delegate someone to de-bone the quails for you, then it is actually quite simple and stress free.

6 quails, de-boned except for the wings and legs
500g (2¾ cups) mixed wild and long grain rice
2–3 pieces chicken liver
½ onion, chopped
150ml (⅔ cup) Madeira
100ml (½ cup) port wine
600ml (2⅓ cups) veal stock/quail stock *(see page 85)*
50g (3½ tablespoons) butter
salt and pepper
vegetable galette or fried bread, to serve
carrots and baby onions, caramelized, to serve
a sprig of parsley, to serve

De-bone the quails. Using a small sharp knife, put your hand inside the carcass of the quail and slowly detach the ribcage from the flesh. Try not to use the knife if possible and work your way through the whole inside of the bird. You will eventually almost turn the bird inside out. Try not to cut into any of the skin, as the bird must be kept whole for stuffing. You may de-bone the night before and stuff the birds the next day.

Cook the wild and long grain rice according to instructions in the package. Do not overcook as it will cook further in the oven. While the rice is cooking, fry the chopped onions in butter until slightly softened, then add in the chopped chicken liver. Again do not overcook. Mix the onions and liver into the rice. Lightly season with salt and pepper.

Season the birds inside and outside. Stuff the birds with the rice mixture. Tie the birds securely with string. Fry the birds all over until golden brown in frying pan with butter. Set oven at 190°C (375°F) and roast the quails for 45 minutes.

Meanwhile, boil Madeira and port down by half, add in the veal or quail stock *(for stock see page 85, substitute veal bones with quail bones)* and reduce to half. Beat in the butter just before serving. Serve the quails immediately with a sprig of parsley on top, lots of gravy, caramelised carrots and baby onions. I also suggest serving the quails on a vegetable galette or a piece of fried bread.

Serves 6

Mustard Pork with Cherry Tomatoes

A very homey stew of pork in a lovely mustard and tomato sauce. Serve it either with pasta or hot steaming rice.

3 medium-sized onions
750 g (1–1½ lb) boned shoulder of pork, trimmed
6 tablespoons olive oil
2 level teaspoons fresh rosemary, chopped
25 g (1¾ tablespoons) butter
3 garlic cloves, crushed
4 level tablespoons tomato paste
100 ml (½ cup) dry sherry
1 tablespoon sugar
1 teaspoon flour
450 ml (1¾ cups) chicken stock
2 teaspoons dark soya sauce
salt and ground black pepper
450 g (1 lb) small, dark, flat mushrooms or white button mushrooms, quartered
3 level tablespoons grainy mustard
2 tablespoons crème fraiche
250 g (1⅔ cups) cherry tomatoes
rosemary and flat-leaf parsley, to garnish

Pre-heat the oven to 180°C (355°F).

Quarter the onions. Cut the pork into 2½ cm (1 inch) chunks. Mix the pork with 30 ml (2 tablespoons) oil and the rosemary. Cover and set aside in a cool place for 2 hours.

Heat the butter in a flameproof casserole dish until just beginning to colour. Add the pork in batches and fry to a rich golden brown. Remove with a slotted spoon and set aside. Lower the heat and add the onions. Cook for 5–7 minutes, or until softened and golden. Add the crushed garlic and tomato paste and fry for 2–3 minutes. Pour in dry sherry and bring to a boil, adding the sugar. Simmer to reduce by half.

Blend in the flour, stirring until smooth, then pour in the stock. Bring to a boil. Return the pork to the pan with the soya sauce and seasoning. Simmer for 5 minutes. Cover tightly and cook in oven for 1–1½ hours until tender.

In the meantime, heat the remaining oil in a large frying pan, add the mushrooms and fry briskly for 3–4 minutes. Season and add to the casserole 10 minutes before the end of the cooking time. Stir in the mustard and crème fraiche, return to the boil and then add tomatoes. The sauce should have a rich consistency. Heat through for about 10 minutes. Adjust the seasoning and serve immediately, garnished with rosemary and flat-leaf parsley.

Serves 6

Sea Bass in Lemongrass Cream

It is the delicate cream sauce which complements this fish—you may also substitute with other oily fish, such as salmon or black cod.

Fish
4 sea bass fillets with skin,
or any other oily fish fillet
salt and black pepper
nori (Japanese seaweed) chopped, to garnish
tomato, chopped, to garnish
sprig of parsley, to garnish
vegetable oil, for frying

Cream Sauce
2 stalks of lemongrass, chopped
250 ml (1 cup) *sake* (Japanese rice wine)
250 ml (1 cup) fish stock (chicken stock will also do)
200 ml (¾ cup) double cream
2 pieces of chilli, (optional)

Pre-heat the oven to 180°C (355°F).

Wash the fish fillets and pat dry. Soak the lemongrass in a little hot fish stock. In a saucepan, bring the *sake* and fish stock to a gentle boil, then let it simmer and reduce by half. Add in the lemongrass and cream. Let it simmer. Then strain and adjust seasoning.

When ready to serve, season the sea bass with salt and black pepper. Warm up sauce. Heat vegetable oil in a non-stick frying pan. When hot, pan fry the sea bass fillets skin down over medium heat for about 3 minutes. Then, turn over and fry for another 2 minutes. Transfer sea bass onto baking tray, skin up, and roast in oven for another 8 minutes (depending on size of fish).

Serve fillet in the middle of the plate and pour cream sauce around the fish.
Garnish with some *nori*, tomato and a sprig of parsley.

Serves 4

Caramelised Pork Belly

A family favourite—kids *love* it!

2 onions, peeled and roughly sliced
vegetable oil
700g (1½ lb) belly pork (or good thick pork ribs), cut in 5cm (2 inch) cubes
6 tablespoons thick, dark, sweet soya sauce (Thai or Malaysian)
4 tablespoons sugar
4 tablespoons fish sauce
water
4–6 pieces Chinese lettuce, to serve
rice, cooked, to serve

Sauté the sliced onions in a little vegetable oil until softened, but not brown. Transfer to heavy saucepan. Brown the pork pieces briskly on high heat, then transfer to saucepan, draining the oil. Add in sweet soya sauce, sugar and fish sauce. Add water until it covers all the meat. Bring to a boil, then let simmer with cover for at least 1 hour. Remove cover and let simmer until the pork is tender and appears glazed. Add water if it dries up, but there should be just enough sauce to coat the meat. The sauce should boil down to a rich dark glaze.

Serve on a bed of Chinese lettuce with a scoop of steaming hot rice.

Serves 6

Simply Roast Duck

This is one of the easiest recipes and is so rewarding. Just make sure you get a nice fattish duck! A frozen duck from the USA or France always works wonders.

one 2¼ kg (4–5 lb) duck
plenty of salt and pepper
250 ml (1 cup) red wine
500 ml (2 cups) chicken or duck stock

Pre-heat the oven to 220°C (430°F).

Season the duck with salt and pepper. Pierce the outer skin of the duck with a sharp needle or small knife all over, so that the fat is released during cooking.

Put the duck in the upper half of the oven. Bring the heat down to 190°C (375°F) after ½ hour and cook for another 2½ hours, periodically removing fat from the tray. Try not to open the oven door too often, as it will release the heat and bring the temperature down.

When duck is golden and crispy, remove from tray and let it rest on serving plate. Meanwhile, de-glaze the tray with red wine. Mix the de-glazed liquid with 2 cups of duck or chicken stock and mix in seasoning of salt and pepper. Boil down and serve with the duck.

Note: each time you have a carcass from poultry, make a stock with carrots, celery, onions and tomatoes and keep in freezer. It always comes in handy.

Serve roast duck with apple sauce (ready or homemade), red cabbage, brussel sprouts and roast potatoes.

Alternatively, you may want to stuff the duck with a chestnut and sausage stuffing, or a wild rice stuffing (*see the wild rice stuffing recipe on page 73 for Stuffed Quail*).

Chestnut and Sausage Stuffing
450 g (1 lb) pork sausage meat
350 g (12 oz) chestnut purée
1 onion, chopped
225 g (8 oz) apples, peeled, cored and chopped
50 g (½ cup) breadcrumbs
1 egg, beaten
salt and pepper

Bind all ingredients and mix well.

Serves 4–6

Gratin of Squash with Tomatoes, Cream and Gruyère Cheese

A meal in itself; perfect for vegetarians or as an accompaniment to a roast or meat dish. Any pumpkin or squash will work for this dish.

1¼ kg (2¾ lbs) squash
4 tablespoons olive oil
1 small onion, finely chopped
2 garlic cloves, crushed
120 ml (½ cup) dry white wine
1 teaspoon sugar
2–3 fresh thyme sprigs, leaves picked, plus extra to garnish (optional)
1 bay leaf
1 tablespoon tomato paste
a pinch of dried chilli flakes
450 g (1 lb) vine-ripened tomatoes, peeled, deseeded and chopped
150 ml (½ cup) double cream
a pinch of nutmeg, grated
100 g (1 cup) gruyère cheese, finely grated

Pre-heat the oven to 180°C (355°F).

Cut the squash into quarters and remove the peel, seeds and fibres. Cut into small, chunky pieces. You should have about 750 g (1 lb 10 oz).

Heat 2 tablespoons of the olive oil in a medium-sized pan, then add the onion and garlic and cook gently until the onion is soft, but not browned. Add the wine and sugar and simmer until reduced by half. Add the thyme, bay leaf, chilli flakes, tomato paste and tomatoes and leave to simmer gently for 15 minutes until reduced and thickened. Season to taste. Discard the bay leaf and spoon the sauce into the base of a shallow ovenproof dish.

Heat the rest of the oil in a large pan, then add the squash and sauté gently for 3–4 minutes, until lightly golden. Scatter the squash over the tomato sauce.

In a small pan, bring the cream and a little grated nutmeg to the boil, again season to taste, but remember that the cheese is quite salty. Remove from the heat.

Sprinkle the cheese over the top of the squash, pour over the cream and bake for 30 minutes until the squash is tender and the cheese is golden and bubbling.

Serves 4 as a main course

Roast Beef Fillet Stuffed with Foie Gras

If you love a good piece of beef, you will love this very rich and decadent dish!

1–2 rolls beef fillet, about 7.5 cm (3 inch)
in diameter or 900 g (2 lb)
300 g (10½ oz) pâté de foie gras,
cut into sticks of 1 cm (½ inch) diameter
(keep cold in freezer for ½ hour)
salt and black pepper
300 ml (1¼ cups) veal stock (see below)
150 ml (⅔ cup) Madeira
50 ml (3 tablespoons) brandy
75 g (5 tablespoons) butter

Veal Stock
2–4 kg (4–8 lbs) veal or chicken bones
500 g (1lb) carrots, chopped
750 g (1½ lbs) onions, chopped
2 celery sticks, chopped
3 leeks, chopped
750 g (1½ lbs) tomatoes, chopped
500 ml (2 cups) dry white wine
1 bay leaf
1 bouquet garni
water

Pre-heat the oven to 190°C (375°F).

Use a thick, rounded, long stick, like a knife sharpener, to pierce a 1 cm (½ inch) hole through the fillet. Stuff the hole with foie gras. You might find that it will start getting mushy, but ensure the hole is filled entirely—we do not want any guest to find their portion with less foie gras!

Season the fillet with salt and black pepper. In a hot pan, heat up oil until sizzling, sear the fillet, browning all sides (including the ends), sealing the juice. Roast fillet for 20 minutes for rare and 30 minutes for medium-rare.

Remove fillet, cut into 2½ cm (1 inch) thick pieces and serve immediately. Watch the foie gras oozing out while slicing the fillet. Scoop up any foie gras that falls out—do not waste any!

Serve immediately with the Madeira sauce.

Veal Stock
The king base of all gravies. Ask your butcher for some veal bones (or a few pieces of osso buco). Heat cooking oil, add in a little flour, stirring until browned. Add in chopped onions, celery, carrots and leek. Stir over medium heat until the vegetables start to release their natural aromas. Brown the bones, then mix together with the vegetables and roast in a pre-heated oven at 180°C (355°F) for 45 minutes. Put ingredients in a large saucepan and add water to cover. Add the white wine, bay leaf and bouquet garni. Bring to a boil, then let simmer for 4–5 hours. Strain the stock and let it boil down to about 1 litre (4 cups). The stock base is now ready. Freeze it in small quantities.

Madeira Sauce
Place 50 g (3½ tablespoons) butter in a small saucepan and cook over a gentle heat until it turns nutty colour (about 20 minutes). Set aside. Melt 25 g (1¾ tablespoons) butter in a pan, add in 150 ml (9 tablespoons) of medium or dry Madeira and 50 ml (3 tablespoons) brandy. Bring to a boil and reduce by half, taking care not to let it burst into flames. Add in the veal stock and seasoning. Finally beat in the browned butter.

Serves 6–8

Beef Rendang with Udon

This is another family recipe that has been passed down from my mum. Beef rendang is a Malaysian dish and is usually served with rice. I find the texture of udon noodles a superior alternative, especially when the sauce coats the long noodles as they slide into your mouth—yum!

900 g (2 lb) beef, shin and tendon
1 bottle thick coconut cream
600 g (1 lb 5 oz) udon noodles (packed or fresh, if possible)

Ground ingredients
3 teaspoons *ketumber* (coriander) powder
12 small shallots
4 cloves garlic
1 piece ginger, about thumb size
4 *buah keras* (candlenuts)
4 fresh chillies (deseeded)
1 piece *kunjit* or 1 teaspoon *kunjit* (saffron) powder
1 stalk lemongrass (bruised)
1 piece crushed *lengkuas* (Thai ginger)
3 lemon leaves
6 *salam* leaves, Indonesian bay leaves
2½ cm (1 inch) piece *asam* (tamarind) diluted with 1 cup water
oil, to sauté ground ingredients
½ teaspoon salt
½ teaspoon sugar

Gently sauté all the ground ingredients in a little vegetable oil. Add in the coconut cream and the *asam* water to the pan and cook for 5 minutes. Add salt, sugar and leaves. Bring to boil, then let simmer.

Meanwhile, brown the beef shin and tendon. Place the beef pieces in the pan to cook, stirring at intervals of 5 minutes until almost all of the liquid is absorbed and the meat is tender. This will take over 1 hour. If the meat is still not tender, add water and cook until ready.

Serve on a bed of freshly cooked udon noodles. Cook udon noodles according to instructions on package. Sprinkle generously with deep-fried shallots and with coriander leaves.

Serves 6

Pan-fried Loin of Lamb with Roasted Butternut Squash and Salsa Verde

A colourful dish that looks great when entertaining, and it is so easy to prepare.

Lamb and Butternut Squash
allow ½ loin (or cannon) of lamb per person,
approximately 150 g (9 oz) — the meat should be
2½ cm (1 inch) thick
2 medium-sized butternut squash
7–8 sprigs rosemary
8 whole cloves garlic, unpeeled
250 ml (1 cup) chicken stock
2 tablespoons olive oil
salt and pepper

Salsa Verde
½ cup–1 cup each of mint, basil and
flat-leaf parsley
1 tablespoon capers with a little of the juice
1 tablespoon Dijon mustard
1 tablespoon balsamic vinegar
2–3 anchovies
125 ml (½ cup) extra-virgin olive oil
½ teaspoon salt
½ teaspoon sugar

Purée all the salsa verde ingredients together in a food processor. Place in a jar and refrigerate until ready to use. It can be stored for up to a week. (Salsa verde is an incredibly useful item to have in the fridge. It's great with anything grilled, with salads or soup — even with goat's cheese on toast).

Pre-heat the oven to 180°C (355°F). Peel the squash and cut them into 5 cm (2 inch) chunks, discarding the seeds. Place the chunks into a roasting dish, toss them with the olive oil, salt and pepper, and scatter the whole garlic cloves and the sprigs of rosemary among them. Place the dish in the oven and roast for approximately 45 minutes, turning the pieces of squash from time to time to ensure that they don't stick to the bottom of the pan and that they brown evenly. When the squash is golden brown and soft, remove from the oven and set aside.

Meanwhile, heat a tablespoon of olive oil in a frying pan over a medium heat. Season the lamb with salt and pepper, and place the lamb into the hot oil. Depending on the size of the pan, you should be able to cook 2 or 3 pieces at a time, but don't overcrowd the pan, as the meat will not brown evenly. Cook the meat for 3–4 minutes on one side (leave the meat alone — do not be tempted to play with it as this only prevents it from browning and encourages it to stick). Then, turn and brown the other side for a further 3–4 minutes. Remove and leave to rest, wrapped in foil, in a warm place for 10 minutes or so.

To make a little 'jus' for the meat, de-glaze the pan with the chicken stock, allowing it to bubble and reduce. Season with salt and pepper and set aside.

To serve, slice the lamb on the diagonal. Place several pieces of squash and roasted garlic cloves in the centre of each plate. Lay the lamb on top and spoon a little of the lamb 'jus' over the pieces. Either spoon over the salsa verde or drizzle around the side of the plate. Serve immediately.

Serves 4

Shin of Veal in Mustard Sauce

Everybody loves osso buco, but this mustard sauce gives it a sophisticated twist!

Veal
4 pieces veal shin
salt and pepper
1 tablespoon plain (all-purpose) flour
oil for frying
4 medium carrots, diced
2 medium onions, diced
2 sticks medium-sized celery, diced
4 cloves of garlic
1 bay leaf
2 sprigs fresh thyme
1 small strip orange zest
300 ml (1¼ cups) dry white wine
300 ml (1¼ cups) Madeira
500 ml (2 cups) chicken stock
a sprig of chervil, to garnish
1 small carrot, diced, to garnish

Mustard Sauce
40 g (3 tablespoons) butter
1 onion, thinly sliced
2 cloves garlic, finely chopped
a sprig of fresh thyme
1 small bay leaf
10 white peppercorns, crushed
200 ml (¾ cup) dry white wine
200 ml (¾ cup) stock, chicken or veal
(see page 85)
1 tablespoon English mustard
2 tablespoons Dijon mustard
500 ml (2 cups) double cream
a dash of lemon juice
1 tablespoon coarse-grain mustard
salt

Pre-heat the oven to 180°C (355°F).

Season the veal with salt and pepper and dust with flour. In a heavy ovenproof pan, fry the meat in a little oil until golden on all sides. Set aside. Add the carrots, onions, celery, herbs and orange zest to the casserole and cook until lightly coloured. Add the white wine and the Madeira. Reduce by half. Add the stock. Return the veal to the pan and cover the pan with a sheet of greaseproof paper. Cut a small hole in the middle. Cook for 2½–3 hours.

To make the mustard sauce, melt the butter in a heavy saucepan. Add the onion, garlic, thyme, bay leaf and peppercorns, cooking until the onion is soft, but not browned. Add the wine and reduce to about 1 tablespoon. Add the stock and reduce by half. Add the English and Dijon mustards and the cream. Bring to a boil. Season with salt and a little lemon juice. Pass through a muslin or sieve. Just before serving, stir in the coarse-grain mustard and check the seasoning.

Remove the meat from the liquid and keep warm. Pass the braising liquid through a fine sieve. In a clean pan, reduce the liquid to a consistency which allows you to glaze the veal. Heat the mustard sauce. When ready to serve, pour some mustard sauce onto the base of the plate or pasta plate. Place a glazed veal shin in the middle. Garnish with diced carrot cubes and a sprig of chervil.

Serves 4

THIRDS

WITH A LITTLE PLANNING AND A WONDERFUL RECIPE, COOKING IS A LOT OF FUN—AND IT BRINGS FAMILY AND FRIENDS TOGETHER. **DOMINICA**

Sticky Toffee Pudding with Toffee Sauce

Who can resist a warm sticky toffee pudding with plenty of sauce? This one is quite light and, depending on the amount of sauce you pour on, not too sweet.

Pudding
200g (7 oz) dates, pitted
375ml (1½ cups) water
6 tablespoons unsalted butter, softened
80g (⅓ cup) packed dark brown sugar
3 large eggs
1½ teaspoons pure vanilla extract
190g (1½ cups) self-rising flour
1½ teaspoons baking soda

Sauce
250ml (1 cup) heavy cream
100g (½ cup) unsalted butter
115g (½ cup) packed dark brown sugar
1 tablespoon golden syrup (preferably Lyle's)

To serve
vanilla ice cream

Pre-heat the oven to 200°C (390°F).

Butter and flour a 23 x 30cm (9 x 12 inch) rectangular baking tin, knocking out excess flour. Combine dates and water in a saucepan and bring to a boil. Cool to room temperature.

Beat butter and brown sugar in a medium bowl with an electric beater until pale and fluffy. Add eggs one at a time, beating well after each addition, then beat in vanilla. Mix in flour.

Purée cooled date mixture with baking soda in a food processor until just blended. Add to batter and stir until just combined. Pour into baking tin, bake until a wooden pick or skewer inserted in the centre of the pudding comes out clean; 20–30 minutes. Cool pudding on a rack for 10 minutes.

To make the sauce, combine cream, butter, brown sugar and syrup in a heavy saucepan and bring to a boil, stirring. Boil until sauce is reduced to about 320ml (1⅓ cups) and thick enough to coat back of a wooden spoon, 3–5 minutes.

Cut pudding into squares, drizzle generously with sauce and serve warm with vanilla ice cream.

Makes about 16 squares

Ice-Cream Crumble with Fresh Raspberry Sauce

An alternative to the usual cooked fruit crumble. Exceptionally easy to make and serve.

Crumble Topping
150g (1¼ cups) plain (all-purpose) flour
65g (¾ cup) almonds, ground with skin
60g (⅓ cup) soft brown sugar
1 packet of 7.5g (2 teaspoons) vanilla sugar or 1 teaspoon vanilla extract
120g (½ cup) unsalted butter, melted
1 teaspoon cinnamon
rind of ½ a lemon

Raspberry Sauce
300g (2½ cups) raspberries
100g (½ cup) granulated sugar

To serve
vanilla ice cream

Pre-heat the oven to 180°C (355°F).

To make the crumble topping, mix all the dry ingredients together. Melt the butter and slowly add it to the dry ingredients until small clumps form. Spread the mixture in a baking tray and bake until golden (about 20 minutes). Take out and cool slightly before breaking into pieces.

Meanwhile, make the raspberry sauce by combining the raspberries and the sugar in a blender and blend until smooth. Force through a fine mesh sieve into a bowl, pressing down firmly on the raspberries. Discard the solids.

To serve, scoop vanilla ice cream into a glass or bowl, sprinkle with the crumble topping and pour raspberry sauce over.

Serves 4–6

Caramelised Pear Tarte Tatin

This tart always looks impressive, yet is so easy to make. If you are uncomfortable about poaching the pears, simply use apples and skip the 'poaching' step.

Pastry
110g (1 cup) plain flour
55g (4 tablespoons) unsalted butter, cut into 1cm (½ inch) cubes

Tarte
4–5 semi-ripe pears (fully ripe pears are too soft and juicy)
110g (⅔ cup) soft dark brown sugar
1 teaspoon ground cinnamon

Pre-heat the oven to 180ºC (355ºF).

Make the shortcrust pastry. Sift flour and rub in the butter with your fingers. When mixture resembles breadcrumbs, knead into dough with the help of a drizzle of cold water, if necessary. Put dough in fridge and let it settle for 20 minutes.

Grease a 20cm (8 inch) baking tin. Cut a circle of greaseproof paper to line the bottom of the tin and grease. Lay the brown sugar evenly over the base of the prepared tin, sprinkle the cinnamon on top. Peel the pears and poach them for a few minutes in some sugared water, and let cool. Core the pears and slice into ½cm (¼ inch) segments. Arrange the slices over the sugar in a circular pattern, starting from the centre, slowly working outwards towards the edge, overlapping a little until all the pear pieces are used.

Take out the dough and roll out to fit over the top of the pears. Press only gently over. Bake for 30 minutes until pastry is a golden brown. When done, let it cool completely before attempting to turn it out as the caramel needs to solidify at room temperature.

When ready to serve, carefully turn the tart upside down onto a serving plate. The idea is to keep the pastry dry on top until just before serving. Gently remove the greaseproof paper. Serve at room temperature with vanilla ice cream or freshly whipped cream.

Serves 6–8

Spicy Sour Cherry Oatmeal Rounds

I love oatmeal cookies and this recipe comes from my mother. They are my absolute favourite.
I personally omit the nuts, but they are delicious with or without!

125 g (1 cup) plain (all-purpose) flour
½ teaspoon baking powder
½ teaspoon ground cinnamon
¼ teaspoon baking soda
¼ teaspoon salt
120 g (½ cup) butter, softened
130 g (⅔ cup) granulated sugar
½ teaspoon vanilla extract
1 egg
65 g (⅔ cup) quick-cooking rolled oats
125 g (1 cup) dried sour cherries or dried cranberries
60 g (½ cup) walnuts, finely chopped (optional)

Pre-heat the oven to 190ºC (375ºF).

In a bowl stir together flour, baking powder, cinnamon, baking soda and salt. Set aside.

In a mixer bowl, beat butter and sugar until well combined and blend in vanilla. Add the egg and beat until fluffy. Gradually blend in flour mixture until well combined. Stir in rolled oats, cranberries and walnuts (if using).

Divide dough in half; transfer each half to a sheet of waxed paper or plastic wrap. Using a spatula and the paper, shape each half into a 5 cm (2 inch)-diameter log. Wrap each log tightly. Refrigerate until firm — at least 2 hours (or place in freezer for 30–45 minutes), or overnight.

Cut logs into ¼ inch-thick slices; arrange slices, slightly apart, on lightly greased baking sheets. Bake until cookies are golden (8–10 minutes). Transfer to wire racks to cool.

Makes about 4 dozen cookies

Shortcake with Berries and Meringue

One of those recipes you can prepare in advance and simply assemble before serving.
The shortcake pastry adds a different touch.

Pastry
6 large egg yolks
120 g (⅔ cup) castor sugar
120 g (½ cup) unsalted butter (leave out to soften)
175 g (1⅓ cups) strong bread flour
1½ teaspoons baking powder

Meringues
(You may use ready-made ones)
2 egg whites
175 g (1 cup) castor sugar
1 teaspoon distilled vinegar
1 teaspoon cornflour

Decoration and Coulis
250 g (1¾ cups) ripe strawberries, hulled
300 g (2 cups) wild strawberries
(regular strawberries will also do)
120 g (1 cup) raspberries
50 g (¼ cup) blackberries or blackcurrants
50 g (¼ cup) blueberries
1 tablespoon castor sugar
a squeeze of lemon
2 tablespoons thick double cream

Pre-heat the oven to 150°C (300°F).

To make the shortcake dough, beat the egg yolks with the sugar until creamy and thick, then gradually beat in the butter. Sift the flour and baking powder together, and mix in. Knead gently into a very soft and wet dough. Wrap in cling film and chill for at least 30 minutes.

Roll out the dough to a thickness of ½ cm (¼ inch) on a lightly floured table top or board. Place on a non-stick baking tray. Prick the dough a few times with a fork. Pinch the centre to make a slight dip, and then pinch the edges into a slight rim. Chill for 30 minutes.

Sprinkle the rolled out dough with a little sugar and bake for 20 minutes until pale golden. Let it sit for a few minutes to firm up, then use a palette knife to help slide it onto a plate to cool and crisp. The shortcake is now ready and can be kept for a day before use.

To make the meringues, whisk egg whites until stiff. Then add in sugar, cornflour and vinegar. Use a tablespoon and scoop individual meringue dollops onto a greased baking paper on baking sheet. Bake in a slow oven at 110°C (230°F) for 50 minutes, and let them cool in the oven.

To make the strawberry coulis, process the hulled strawberries to a purée. Add sugar to taste, plus a squeeze of lemon juice and the double cream.

When ready to serve, assemble the shortcake. Coat the surface with a layer of coulis. Decorate with the berries and finish off with the mini meringues on top (or crush them a little). After serving a slice, drizzle some coulis around the plate.

Serves 8

Apple Parcels

Another easy recipe that is always a success.

Filling
3–4 apples
unsalted butter
1 teaspoon cinnamon
1 teaspoon castor sugar or light brown sugar
4–6 slices sandwich bread
vanilla ice cream, to serve

Batter
4 eggs
4 tablespoons castor sugar
4 tablespoons double cream
50 g (3½ tablespoons) butter

Core and peel the apples. Cut the apples into 1 cm (½ inch) cubes. Heat up a small knob of butter in a saucepan and, on low heat, cook the apple cubes until they begin to soften, mixing in cinnamon and sugar. Leave to cool.

Butter the sandwich bread on one side only. Place some apple pieces on one half of the triangle, leaving a rim on the edge. Fold the bread over making a triangle parcel and press on the edges to seal. Cut off the crusts and ensure the parcels are firmly sealed. Make one per guest.

Make the batter with the eggs, sugar, double cream and butter, mixing well together.

Dip the sandwich parcels into the batter until thoroughly soaked. Make sure the edges are firmly sealed. Heat up butter in frying pan. Fry the battered parcels in the butter until golden brown on both sides.

Sprinkle the turnovers with some castor sugar. Serve with a scoop of vanilla ice cream.

Serves 4–6

Tarte Au Citron

If you love the tangy taste of lemon custard that melts in your mouth, you will not be able to say no to this delicious recipe.

Pastry
1 egg
75g (⅓ cup) castor sugar
110g (½ cup) unsalted butter (keep cool)
275g (2¾ cups) plain flour
a pinch of salt
vanilla ice cream or thick cream, to serve

Filling
110g (½ cup) unsalted butter
175g (1 cup) sugar
4 eggs, beaten
3 tablespoons crème fraiche
4 tablespoons lemon or three-fruit marmalade
rind and juice of 3 lemons
rind of 1 orange

To make the pastry, beat egg with castor sugar until it is creamy and light. Sift in the flour with a pinch of salt and mix into the egg mixture with a wooden spoon until it resembles coarse breadcrumbs. Cut the butter into small cubes in the mixture and use your fingertips to rub in the butter. You might find the mixture quite sticky if working in a humid or warm room. Work the mixture into a dough and wrap in cling film. Set aside in fridge.

Note: you can always make the pastry dough in advance and also bake the pastry a day in advance.

Pre-heat the oven to 190°C (375°F).

Flour your work table generously. Knead the dough a few times with your knuckles. Roll out the pastry on the floured surface, turning the pastry over constantly, and making sure the table surface and rolling pin are floured. Roll out the pastry to a thickness of 1cm (½ inch). Grease a 23cm (9 inch) pastry tin and line it with the pastry, making sure the edge is a little over the tin. This is a very buttery pastry, so do not despair if the pastry seems a little too sticky to roll out to perfection. Use a knife and trim off any excess pastry over rim of the tin.

Set pastry aside in fridge for 15 minutes before baking. This is essential, as it will prevent the tart from shrinking during baking. Bake the tart blind for 20 minutes (line the tart with greaseproof paper and fill it with uncooked rice or beans, removing the greaseproof paper and rice/beans for the last 5 minutes). Set aside and cool.

To make the filling, cream the butter and the sugar until light and fluffy. Slowly add the beaten egg, stopping once in a while to scrape down the side and bottom of the mixture. Then add in the crème fraiche, marmalade, lemon and orange rind. Slowly mix in the lemon juice, but do not add in all the lemon juice, depending on the size of the lemons. Taste the mixture and adjust the tanginess according to your taste. The mixture might curdle at this point but it will not affect the outcome of the tart. Pour mixture into the cooled tart shell and bake in pre-heated oven of 170°C (340°F) for 45–50 minutes until the centre of the tart is set and a little wobbly. Take tart out and cool.

To decorate the tart, sprinkle icing sugar over the top. Place a slice of lemon or lime in the centre. This tart tastes great with vanilla ice cream or some thick cream.

Serves 8

Bittersweet Chocolate Mousse

I have tried lots of recipes, but this one for chocolate mousse stands out as the winner.

150 g (5½ oz) bittersweet chocolate, finely grated or chopped
2 tablespoons unsalted butter, softened
4 large eggs, separated
1 tablespoon vanilla sugar
60 ml (¼ cup) heavy cream, chilled
6 tablespoons icing sugar

Melt the chocolate together with the butter, either by placing the chocolate and butter in the top of a double boiler set over gently simmering water (do not cover the pan, or drops of water will drip into the chocolate and alter its texture), or in a microwave oven, being careful not to heat too long.

In the bowl of an electric mixer, beat the egg yolks and vanilla sugar until thick and lemon coloured. Whisk this into the cooled chocolate mixture until thoroughly blended.

Whip the cream until stiff. With a rubber spatula, fold the whipped cream into the chocolate mixture until thoroughly blended. Set aside.

Combine the egg whites and icing sugar in the electric mixer bowl, and whisk until stiff but not dry. Fold one third of the egg whites into the chocolate mixture and combine thoroughly, then gently fold in the remaining whites. Do not over mix, but be sure that the mixture is well blended and that no streaks of egg white remain. Transfer to a 1 litre (4 cups) serving bowl or individual glasses, cover, and refrigerate for at least 1 hour before serving.

Serves 6–8

Berry Summer Pudding

A stress-free recipe to be made two days in advance—just unveil when it is dessert time.

225 g (1¾ cups) raspberries
275 g (2 cups) redcurrants, blackcurrants, blueberries
275 g (2 cups) strawberries
110 g (½ cup) castor sugar
120 ml (8 tablespoons) water
8–10 slices of two-day-old white bread
double cream, to serve

In a large saucepan, combine all the fruit except raspberries (as they cook too quickly) with 8 tablespoons of water. Bring to a simmer and cook over low heat for a few minutes, stirring gently once or twice. Do not overcook the fruits as they will become mushy and soft. Add in the raspberries and then the sugar and stir until the sugar has dissolved. Remove from heat and let it cool.

Trim crusts off the bread. Line the bottom and the side of a 1 litre (4 cups) pudding bowl with the bread slices, making sure they overlap a little so there are no gaps. You might want to cut them to fit neatly. Pour the fruit and most of the juices into the lined bowl and top with a layer of bread, making sure to cover the diameter of the bowl. Spoon the remaining juice over the pudding, making sure all the bread is soaked.

Invert a plate small enough to fit just inside the top of the basin over the bread and weigh it down. Put the bowl on a plate as some juice might overflow. Keep pudding in the refrigerator for 2 days.

When ready to serve, remove weight and plate from pudding. Gently run a knife around the inside of the basin loosening the bread on the side. Gently invert the pudding onto a serving platter. Spoon any juices from the bowl over the top of the pudding. Decorate with fresh berries. As you spoon out the pudding for each guest, the glorious juicy berries will ooze out. Serve with double cream.

Serves 6–8

Linzertorte

This is a very special recipe as it was given to me by my mother, whose mother gave it to her. This is a true Austrian Linzertorte!

150 g (1½ cups) flour
150 g (¾ cup) castor sugar
150 g (1 cup) almonds or hazelnuts toasted, skinned and cooled
150 g (⅔ cup) butter
1 teaspoon baking powder
1 packet of 7.5 g (2 teaspoons) vanilla sugar
1 egg and 1 egg yolk
¼ teaspoon cloves
½ teaspoon cinnamon
¼ teaspoon salt
125 g (1 cup) raspberry jam
zest of 1 lemon
whipped cream, to serve

Put a rack in middle of oven and pre-heat the oven to 190°C (375°F).

Pulse nuts in a food processor until finely ground; do not grind to a paste. Mix together the flour, baking powder, spices and sugars. Blend in the butter either with your fingertips or in a food processor until the mixture resembles coarse breadcrumbs. Add the nuts and mix. Then add the egg and egg yolk to the mixture until the dough just holds together. Divide dough in half and form each half into a disk. Wrap disks in plastic wrap and refrigerate until firm (about 30 minutes).

Line bottom of a round 25 cm (10 inch) spring-form pan with a round of parchment paper. Press 1 disk of dough evenly onto bottom and ¼ inch up sides of spring-form pan, using the back of a large spoon to smooth it if necessary. Spread jam evenly onto dough base.

Roll out remaining dough between two sheets of wax paper into a 25 cm (10 inch) round, 1 cm (½ inch) thick. Remove top sheet of paper and cut dough into twelve 1 cm (½ inch) wide strips. Arrange remaining strips perpendicular to first strips to form a simple lattice. Crimp and seal edges with a fork.

Bake torte until lattice is lightly browned, about 35 minutes. Cool completely on a rack (about 2 hours) before serving. Serve with a dollop of freshly whipped cream.

Serves 8–12

Fruit Tempura with Passionfruit Ice-Cream

One of those hot and cold sensations. The ice cream is great even served on its own.

Fruit Tempura
125 g (¾ cup) rice flour
250 ml (1 cup) light beer
300 ml (1¼ cups) water
1 large egg yolk
2 large egg whites
4–5 different pieces of fruit per person,
cut to 3 cm (1½ inch) squares
(pineapple, apple, banana, plum or firm pear)
juice of 1 lemon
sunflower oil
icing or vanilla sugar

Passionfruit Ice Cream
1 litre (4 cups) single cream
5 egg yolks
250 g (1¼ cups) castor sugar
4–6 passionfruit, pulp and seeds
2 tablespoons Grand Marnier (optional)

Mango Coulis
2 ripe mangoes, peeled and cored
75 g (⅔ cup) icing sugar, sifted
water

For the batter, put the rice flour in a mixing bowl. Add in the beer and water. Beat using a large balloon whisk until smooth. Then beat in the egg yolk. Toss the sliced fruit in lemon juice to prevent discolouration. I would suggest 4–5 pieces per serving.

Note: if you don't have time to make your own batter, the ready-made tempura batter mix is just as good and stress-free.

When ready to cook, whisk the egg whites in a bowl until stiff but soft, fold in the batter using a large metal spoon. Fill up a heavy, deep saucepan to a third with sunflower oil. Heat to a temperature of 180°C (355°F). Take a piece of fruit, dust it with icing sugar, then dip it quickly in the batter to coat lightly and place in the hot oil. Fry for about 2 minutes until golden and crisp. Continue frying the fruit pieces in small batches, and leave to drain on kitchen towels. Only dip the fruit in the batter just before frying. Transfer to a low oven to keep warm whilst waiting to fry the other fruit pieces.

For the passionfruit ice cream, pour the cream into a saucepan and heat gently. Beat the egg yolks and sugar together in a bowl until pale and creamy. Beat 2 tablespoons of the hot cream into the egg mixture, then beat in the remaining cream, little by little. Put in a bowl over simmering water and cook over gentle heat, stirring constantly, until the mixture coats the back of the spoon.

Let the mixture cool. Then stir in the passionfruit pulp, seeds and juice. Mix well. Add the liqueur. Churn in an ice cream machine for 50 minutes. Transfer to a container and freeze. Leave out for a few minutes before serving.

To make the mango coulis, carefully peel and core the mangoes. Slice into small pieces and put in blender together with 75 g (⅔ cup) icing sugar. Blend until smooth. Add a little water to adjust consistency. Keep the coulis in an airtight container in the refrigerator until ready to use.

Serve fruit tempura immediately with a generous scoop of passionfruit ice cream and mango coulis. Dust with icing or vanilla sugar.

Serves 4

Chocolate Mousse Layer Cake

The candied orange peel, chocolate mousse and Cointreau in the cake makes this a deadly but unforgettable experience. It takes a little time to make but it tastes out of this world! I make it once a year for my Christmas Tea. The chocolate mousse could be served on its own; just let it set in your serving bowl in the fridge.

Cake
150 g (5½ oz) marzipan
40 g (⅓ cup) icing sugar, sifted
5 eggs, separated
25 g (4 tablespoons) cocoa powder
25 g (3¼ tablespoons) flour
25 g (2½ tablespoons) potato flour
1 tablespoon castor sugar
chocolate sticks or squares, for decoration
fruit and mint leaves, to serve

Mousse
110 g (4 oz) plain chocolate, broken into pieces
55 g (4 tablespoons) butter
2 egg yolks
4 egg whites
40 g (¼ cup) sugar

Cointreau Syrup
60 g (⅓ cup) sugar
90 ml (⅓ cup) water
2 tablespoons Cointreau
25 g (4 tablespoons) candied orange peel

Pre-heat the oven to 170°C (340°F).

To make the chocolate mousse, melt the chocolate in a bain-marie (bowl over hot water). When completely melted, remove from heat and stir in the butter until melted. Mix in the egg yolks. Whisk in the egg whites with the sugar until stiff. Fold into the chocolate mixture. Make sure the meringue is completely folded into the mixture or the mousse will lose its volume.

To make the cake, mix together the marzipan and icing sugar. It will look very dry but don't worry! Add the egg yolks. Sift together the cocoa, flour and potato flour. Add to the marzipan mixture. Whisk the egg whites with the castor sugar to a stiff meringue, then fold into the mixture. Turn the mixture into a greased 17 cm (7 inch)-square baking tin, which has been lined with greaseproof paper. Bake in the oven for 35 minutes. Set aside to cool.

To make the Cointreau syrup, bring sugar and water together to boil in a saucepan, stirring to dissolve the sugar. Remove from the heat and cool. Then add the Cointreau. Chop the candied peel in a food processor and soften with the syrup.

To assemble the cake, cut the cooled cake into three equal layers. Moisten them with the Cointreau syrup. Start with the bottom layer: sprinkle with candied orange peel, then spread the top evenly with chocolate mousse. Put second layer on, then repeat with the candied peel and chocolate mousse. Finally, top with the final layer of cake. Cover the top and sides of the whole cake with mousse and leave to set in the fridge. If possible, leave overnight in fridge to allow the flavours to infuse.

Before serving, decorate the sides and top of the cake with the decorative chocolate. Then dress up the top with some fruit and mint leaves. This recipe can be made the night before.

Serves 8–10

Auntie Car's Lemon Squares

These lemon squares are my daughter's absolute favourite. The recipe comes from my sister-in-law, whose love of desserts provides us with endless treats.

Base
168 g (¾ cup) unsalted butter
125 g (1 cup) plain (all-purpose) flour
45 g (¼ cup) light brown sugar
¼ teaspoon salt

Topping
2 large eggs
150 g (¾ cup) castor sugar
60 ml (¼ cup) lemon juice
3 tablespoons icing sugar

Pre-heat the oven to 180°C (355°F).

To make the base, cut butter into pieces. Mix all ingredients in a food processor until it resembles bread crumbs. Sprinkle mixture in a 23 cm (9 inch)-square greased tin and pat down firmly. Bake in middle of oven until golden, for 20 minutes.

To make the topping, whisk eggs and sugar until well combined and add lemon juice. Pour lemon mixture over hot shortbread. Reduce oven temperature to 170°C (340°F) and bake in oven for 30 minutes. Cool completely in pan and then sift icing sugar over. Cut into squares.

Makes about 16–24 squares

Scones

These are English scones, the kind served at traditional afternoon teas. Homemade scones are so simple to make and much better than the bought variety. Serve them warm with clotted cream and strawberry jam. They are best eaten fresh as they go stale very quickly.

225 g (2 cups) self-raising flour, plus extra
40 g (2¾ tablespoons) butter
3 tablespoons sugar
a pinch of salt
130 ml (½ cup) milk

To serve
clotted cream
strawberry jam

Pre-heat the oven to 220°C (430°F). Grease baking sheet.

Rub butter into the flour until it looks like breadcrumbs. Next stir in the sugar and salt, then use a knife to mix in the milk a little at a time. Flour your hands and knead the mixture to a soft dough. Add a little more milk if it feels dry. Be careful not to over-knead the dough. Alternatively you can make the dough in a food processor.

Turn dough out onto a floured surface and roll or pat out to a thickness of not less than 2 cm (1 inch). Using a 4–5 cm (1½–2 inch) pastry cutter, place it on the dough and with one sharp movement press straight through the dough. Do not twist the cutter or you will not get the beautiful rise of the scone in the oven. Repeat until you have used all the dough. Place the scones on the greased baking tray, dust each one with a little flour and bake near top of oven for 12–15 minutes until a crisp golden-brown. Cool on a wire rack and serve slightly warm, crisp on the outside and soft and fluffy inside.

Makes about 12 scones

Chocoholics Chocolate Gateau

I am always looking for the 'ultimate' chocolate cake recipe. This one couldn't be easier and it never fails to delight. It comes from a book on chocolate quite simply called 'Chocolate', given to me by a friend who knows how much I love cookbooks. It is best made the evening before, if possible.

200 g (7 oz) good-quality dark chocolate
200 g (1 cup) butter
250 g (1¼ cup) sugar
5 eggs
1 tablespoon flour
icing sugar, to serve

Pre-heat the oven to 190ºC (375ºF).

Melt the chocolate and butter in a microwave oven or bain-marie. Add the sugar and leave to cool slightly. Add the eggs one by one to the chocolate mixture, stirring well after adding each one.

Finally, add the flour and stir until well combined. Pour batter into a greased 20 cm (8 inch) diameter baking tin and bake for 22 minutes. The cake should not quite have set in the middle.

Remove from oven and leave to cool and rest. To serve, dust with icing sugar.

Serves 6–8

Fried Apples with Toffee Sauce

Simply delicious and yet SO easy!

Apples
3 apples, peeled and cored
10 g (2 teaspoons) unsalted butter
4 teaspoons clear honey
2–3 tablespoons icing sugar, sifted
2 sprigs of fresh mint

Toffee Sauce
580 ml (2⅓ cups) double cream
75 g (⅓ cup) Demerara sugar
(small brown crystal sugar)
30 ml (2 tablespoons) black treacle

Slice across the apples to make 1 cm (½ inch) pieces. Gently heat butter in a frying pan. Sit the apples in the pan and fry until the apples become a rich brown colour with tinges of burnt edges — this gives a bittersweet apple taste. Turn the apples over and cook for another 1–2 minutes until brown and just tender. Transfer the apple slices onto a greased baking sheet and spoon some honey on top of the apples. Sprinkle some icing sugar through a tea strainer over the top. Finish off by caramelising the sugar with a blowtorch. You may skip this last stage if you find it troublesome — the apples will still taste wonderful.

To make the toffee sauce put all the ingredients into a saucepan, bring to a boil, and then simmer for 10 minutes until reduced.

For a quick alternative to the above, simply sit a tin of condensed milk in a saucepan filled with water and bring to a boil. Let simmer for three hours, making sure the tin is totally submerged in the hot water. Set aside to cool. When cooled, open the tin and there you have ready-made toffee cream. You may adjust the consistency of the cream to your liking by mixing in single or double cream. This is amazingly simple — try it!

To serve, place 3 apple slices onto each plate and serve with thick toffee sauce and a sprig of mint.

Serves 4

Light and Crunchy Flapjacks

I love flapjacks of all sorts, but these are my all-time favourite. The addition of the rice crispies makes the whole thing light and 'crispy'. My thanks to Henrietta for kindly sharing this recipe with me.

120g (½ cup) butter
1 tablespoon golden syrup (preferably Lyle's)
120g (½ cup) castor sugar
90g (1 cup) oats
60g (½ cup) self-raising flour
60g (½ cup) rice crispies

Pre-heat the oven to 200°C (390°F).

Melt butter and golden syrup together. Mix in the sugar, oats, flour and rice crispies. Spread mixture into a 33 x 23cm (13 x 9 inch) baking pan or Pyrex and press down firmly. Bake 15 minutes.

Note: place the tablespoon in hot water before dipping into the golden syrup, as it will help the syrup slide off the spoon smoothly.

Makes about 24 squares

Moist Lemon Cake with Syrupy Lemon Glaze

This lovely afternoon tea cake is even nicer when served still slightly warm from the oven with a dollop of fresh cream.

Cake
185 g (1½ cups) plain (all-purpose) flour
1 teaspoon double acting baking powder
½ teaspoon salt
112 g (½ cup) butter, softened, plus extra for the pan
230 g (1¼ cup) sugar
2 large eggs
125 ml (½ cup) milk
1 teaspoon pure vanilla extract
zest of ½ a lemon

Lemon Syrup
juice of 1 lemon
55 g (¼ cup) castor sugar

Pre-heat the oven to 160°C (320°F).

Line the bottom and sides of a buttered 21 x 10 x 7 cm (8½ x 4 x 2¾ inch) loaf pan with waxed paper. Into a bowl sift together the flour, baking powder and salt. In an electric mixer, cream the butter with the sugar until the mixture is light and fluffy, and add the eggs, one at a time, beating well after each addition. Add the lemon zest. Then add the flour mixture to the butter mixture in batches, alternating with the milk, and blend the batter well.

Spoon the batter into the loaf pan, spreading it evenly, and bake the cake in the middle of the oven for about 1 hour, or until a cake tester comes out clean. Transfer the cake in the pan to a rack.

To make the syrup, combine the lemon juice and sugar in a small saucepan, and heat the mixture over low heat, stirring, until the sugar is dissolved and it becomes slightly syrupy. Brush the syrup over the cake and let the cake cool completely before turning it out of the pan.

Serves 8

Tapioca Brûlée with Coconut, Mango and Pomelo

A great fusion dessert!

400 ml (1¾ cups) canned coconut milk
200 ml (¾ cup) milk
75 g (⅓ cup) castor sugar
75 g (½ cup) tapioca
2 limes
100 ml (½ cup) double cream
2 large, ripe mangoes
4 segments pomelo, shredded
4–6 ripe passionfruits
grated zest of 1 lime
castor sugar, for brûlée

Place the coconut milk and milk in a saucepan over medium heat and bring to just under boiling point. Reduce heat, add the sugar and tapioca. Keep stirring to help the sugar melt and prevent the tapioca from forming lumps. Cook the tapioca until the pearls are almost transparent and softened (about 30–45 minutes, depending on the tapioca you use). When cool, stir in the shredded pomelo. Pour into a bowl and set aside in a cool place.

Zest the limes, cover and set aside. Squeeze the juice from one of the limes. Whip the cream lightly, then add the lime juice to the tapioca and fold in the cream.

Peel the mangoes and cut into small slices or cubes. Place the pieces in a bowl. Scrape the seeds from the passionfruit onto the mango.

Divide the mango between 8–10 ramekins or small heatproof bowls, then cover with the cooled tapioca. The puddings are almost ready now and could be prepared in advance up to this point and kept in the refrigerator overnight.

When ready to serve, bring out the puddings and let them sit at room temperature for 10–15 minutes. Sprinkle the top of the puddings generously and evenly with the castor sugar. Burn the topping with a blowtorch until caramelised. Let the sugar harden at room temperature (about 1–2 minutes). Decorate the top of each ramekin with slivers of lime zest and serve immediately.

Serves 8–10

Irresistible Christmas Cake

I bake about 30–40 Christmas cakes to give to friends every year. The fragrance of Christmas fills the house throughout November, as we bake every week! You can make this any time of the year — it is just a wonderful rich fruit cake.

450 g (1 lb) currants
175 g (6 oz) raisins
175 g (6 oz) sultanas
50 g (2 oz) candied citrus peels, chopped
50 g (2 oz) candied cherries, chopped
8 tablespoons brandy
225 g (1 cup) unsalted butter
½ teaspoon ground mixed spice
¼ teaspoon nutmeg
freshly whipped cream, to serve

225 g (2⅓ cups) plain flour, sifted
a pinch of salt
225 g (1½ cups) soft dark brown sugar
4 large eggs, beaten
3 tablespoons black treacle
zest of 1 lemon
zest of 1 orange
50 g (½ cup) almond flakes, chopped
whipped cream, to serve

Pre-heat the oven at 140ºC (285ºF).

The night before you bake, put all the dried fruits (currants, raisins, sultanas, candied peels and cherries) in a large bowl, pour 8 tablespoons of brandy over and mix well. Cover with a tea towel and let the fruits soak in the brandy.

Line a 20 cm (8 inch) cake tin (or 2 smaller rectangular tins if you wish to bake smaller cakes) with grease-proof paper. Grease the paper with butter. Wrap the sides and bottom of the tin with a double layer of brown paper and tie with string to keep it in place.

Cream butter and brown sugar until fluffy and creamy. Slowly add in the beaten eggs, a tablespoon at a time, still beating. (The mixture could curdle at this point but do not lose heart: it will turn out well!) Fold in the flour and salt, bit by bit, until well mixed. Then gradually fold in the dried fruits, followed by the treacle, zests and almond flakes. Scrape the bottom of the mixing bowl, making sure it is all mixed well. Turn the mixture into the baking tins. Cover the cake with a double layer of greaseproof paper and cut a 2½ cm (1 inch) diameter hole in the middle to let the cake breathe. Bake in the oven for at least 4½ hours, up to 5 hours. Do not attempt to open the oven door for at least 3 hours.

When the cake is done, take it out of the oven and let it cool for about ½ hour. Then, turn it out of the tin with the greaseproof paper to let it cool further. When it has cooled, poke a few holes on top of the cake and pour 1 tablespoon of brandy evenly over the cake. Then wrap it well again and store. The cake is now ready to be fed with a tablespoon of brandy every week, until you wish to serve. The cake can be kept for 4–6 weeks and the weekly tablespoon of brandy will make the cake more mature and delectable. Serve with a dollop of freshly whipped cream.

Serves 10–12